305.8

Islamophobia
issues, challenges and action

A report by the Commission on British Muslims and Islamophobia

Chaired by Dr Richard Stone

Research by Hugh Muir and Laura Smith

Editor: Robin Richardson

Adviser: Imam Dr Abduljalil Sajid

Trentham Books

Stoke on Trent, UK and Sterling, USA

in association with the Uniting Britain Trust, London

Trentham Books Limited

Westview House	22883 Quicksilver Drive
734 London Road	Sterling
Oakhill	VA 20166-2012
Stoke on Trent	USA
Staffordshire	
England ST4 5NP	

First published 2004

British Library Cataloguing-in-Publication Data
A catalogue record for this book is available from the British Library

1 85856 317 8

Designed and typeset by Trentham Print Design Ltd., Chester and printed in Great Britain by Bemrose Shafron (Printers) Ltd, Chester.

CONTENTS

LIST OF BOXES AND TABLES

BACKGROUND AND ACKNOWLEDGEMENTS

Consultations underlying this report

Acknowledgement is due to the many hundreds of people who took part in the projects and activities of the Commission on British Muslims and Islamophobia in the period 1999-2004. There were widespread consultations, conferences and meetings, including events in Birmingham, Bradford, London and Manchester; substantial contacts, meetings and correspondence with interested individuals and organisations; several submissions to government departments; briefing papers for parliamentarians; and the publication, dissemination and discussion of a range of documents. The secretary of the Commission in 1999-2002 was Kaushika Amin.

Documents published by the Commission included an interim report, *Addressing the Challenge of Islamophobia*; a list of resources relating to the events of 11 September 2001, widely circulated in the ensuing weeks; a model policy statement for schools, published on the internet; a booklet about the Race Relations (Amendment) Act, *Changing Race Relations*, published in summer 2002; and a leaflet for teachers and youth workers about the war in Iraq, published in spring 2003.

Throughout the period 1999-2004 the Commission benefited from the advice, support and publications of several Muslim organisations, in particular the Muslim Council of Britain.

Origins

The Commission was set up by the Runnymede Trust in 1996. Its first report, *Islamophobia: a challenge for us all*, was published in 1997 and was launched at the House of Commons by the Home Secretary, Jack Straw MP.

Authorship and editing

Much of the material in this report was researched and assembled by Hugh Muir and Laura Smith. Hugh Muir works for *The Guardian* and was previously at the *Evening Standard*. Laura Smith worked until recently as a journalist at the *Evening Standard* and is now working freelance and studying towards a masters degree at the London School of Economics.

Substantial assistance was provided by a range of Muslim organisations. They included the Muslim Council of Britain and the An-Nisa Society. A co-director of the latter, Khalida Khan, is a member of the Commission.

The report was edited by Robin Richardson. He is a director of the Insted consultancy and a member of the Commission.

The adviser for the report was Imam Dr Abduljalil Sajid. He is chair of the Muslim Council for Religious and Racial Harmony UK and for several years was chair of the social policy, welfare and regeneration committee of the Muslim Council of Britain, and chair or vice-chair of the Joint Council for the Welfare of Immigrants. He has been a member of the Commission on British Muslims and Islamophobia since 1996.

Funding

Throughout the period 1999-2004, up to and including the production of this report, the Commission's work was generously funded by the Stone Ashdown Trust.

Chair

Since 1999 the Commission has been chaired by Dr Richard Stone. He was an adviser to the Stephen Lawrence Inquiry, 1997-1999, and is chair of the Uniting Britain Trust and of the Jewish Council for Racial Equality. He is vice-chair of the Runnymede Trust.

Members

Solma Ahmed, adviser to the Government's Community Housing Task Force

Yousif Al-Khoei, the director of the Al-Khoie Foundation

Dr Kate Gavron, vice-chair of the Runnymede Trust

Professor Ian Hargreaves, professor of media studies at the University of Cardiff

Khalida Khan, director of the An-Nisa Society, London

Dr Philip Lewis, lecturer in peace studies at the University of Bradford

Robin Richardson, co-director of the Insted consultancy

Imam Dr Abduljalil Sajid, chair of the Muslim Council for Religious and Racial Harmony UK

Anil Singh, director of the Manningham Housing Association, Bradford

Selina Ullah, senior manager Bradford Community Health Trust

Revd John Webber, adviser on inter-faith issues to the Bishop of Stepney

Talha Wadee, formerly director of the Lancashire Council of Mosques.

***Pranlal Sheth**, a trustee of the Uniting Britain Trust and of the Runnymede Trust, was a member of the Commission until his death in summer 2003.*

Interviews and assistance

In preparing material for this book Hugh Muir and Laura Smith interviewed Syed Nawazish Bokhari, president of the Muslim Teachers' Association; Basma Elshayyal, head of religious education and citizenship co-ordinator, Islamia School, Queen's Park, London; Golshad Ghiaci, psychotherapist; Humera Khan and Khalida Khan, directors of the an-Nisa Society; Imran Khan, disk jockey and broadcaster; Sadiq Khan , senior lawyer; Shazia Mirza, comedian; Bushra Nasir, headteacher, Plashet School, London, and students at the school; Murad Qureshi, Westminster City Council; Abdullah Trevathan, headteacher, Brondesbury College for Boys, London, and students at the college; the Association of Muslim Schools; Baroness Uddin, House of Lords; Mohammed Umar, publisher; Ahmed Versi, editor of *The Muslim News*; and Rashid Yaqoob, solicitor.

Comments on the report's final draft were received from Tahir Alam (Muslim Council of Britain); Mohammed Abdul Aziz (British Muslim Research Centre); Yahya Birt (Islamic Foundation); Adrian Brockett (York St John College); Inayat Bunglawala (Muslim Council of Britain); Tufyal Chaudhury (University of Durham); Kate Gavron (Runnymede Trust); Elinor Kelly (University of Glasgow), Khalida Khan and Humera Khan (An-Nisa Society); Michelynn Lafleche and colleagues (Runnymede Trust); Philip Lewis (University of Bradford); Maleiha Malik (King's College, London); Tariq Modood (University of Bristol), Iqbal Sacranie (Muslim Council of Britain); and Talha Wadee (formerly Lancashire Council of Mosques).

Views expressed or implied in the text of the report, and any errors, are the responsibility of the Commission on British Muslims and Islamophobia. They are not to be understood as necessarily representing the views or understandings of any other person or organisation above.

The Commission's first phase

In its first phase, leading to the publication of its report in 1997, the Commission was chaired by Professor Gordon Conway, vice-chancellor of the University of Sussex. Its members were:

Maqsood Ahmad, then director of Kirklees Racial Equality Council

Professor Akbar Ahmed, then fellow of Selwyn College, Cambridge

Dr Zaki Badawi, principal of the Muslim College, London

Rt Rev Richard Chartres, Bishop of London

Ian Hargreaves, then editor of the New Statesman and later professor of media studies at the University of Cardiff

Dr Philip Lewis, at that time adviser on inter-faith issues to the Bishop of Bradford and lecturer in religious studies at the University of Leeds and now lecturer in peace studies at the University of Bradford

Zahida Manzoor, chair of the Bradford Health Authority

Rabbi Julia Neuberger, later chief executive of the King's Fund

Trevor Phillips, chair of the Runnymede Trust and later vice-chair of the Greater London Authority and chair of the Commission for Racial Equality

Dr Sebastian Poulter, reader in law at the University of Southampton

Usha Prashar, civil service commissioner

Hamid Qureshi, at that time director of the Lancashire Council of Mosques

Nasreen Rehman, trustee of the Runnymede Trust

Saba Risaluddin, director of the Calamus Foundation

Imam Dr Abduljalil Sajid, chair of the Muslim Council for Religious and Racial Harmony UK

Dr Richard Stone, chair of the Jewish Council for Racial Equality

Revd John Webber, adviser on inter faith issues to the Bishop of Stepney.

FOREWORD

Richard Stone

In the early 1990s the Runnymede Trust established a commission on antisemitism. One of the commissioners, a distinguished Muslim scholar, argued cogently that there are many parallels between anti-Jewish prejudice and anti-Muslim prejudice in modern Britain, and that anti-Muslim prejudice was increasing rapidly and dangerously in force and seriousness. His fellow commissioners agreed with him and in their final report recommended that a broadly similar commission should be established by Runnymede to look at Islamophobia. I was invited to be a member of this.

Our report, *Islamophobia: a challenge for us all*, was launched in 1997 by the new Home Secretary, Jack Straw. With the publication of our report the commission closed down and the commissioners went their various ways. I was occupied throughout most of 1998 as a panel member of the Stephen Lawrence Inquiry. When the Inquiry finished I was dismayed to find that the recommendations of the Islamophobia commission had been largely ignored by local and central government. So I arranged for it to be re-constituted for three years, 1999-2002, under the auspices of the Uniting Britain Trust. A full-time secretary was engaged, Kaushika Amin, and through her we put pressure on public bodies to study our report and to review their practices in the light of it. In this way we intended and expected to keep Islamophobia on the public agenda. This follow-up report draws extensively on the programme of activities and consultations that Kaushika organised.

On 15 February 2003 there took place the biggest public demonstration ever in British history. One of its many characteristics was the sense of shared community. 'Pakistani women shared pakoras and cucumber sandwiches with women from the shires in the biggest anti-war march ever,' wrote a Muslim journalist, 'a postcard image of race relations that no Home Office initiative could even dream of achieving'.

But within weeks, the wonderful solidarity seen on that day seemed to be unravelling. There is now renewed talk of a clash of civilisations, a new global cold war, and mounting concern that the already fragile foothold gained by Muslim communities in Britain is threatened by ignorance and intolerance. 'For most Muslims,' continued the journalist quoted

above, 'the war dramatically exposed how partisan the western media is – and, for many, how crass western politicians are and how gullible the western public is. However, it is the despair, the frustration and the anger that should be noted. Today, Britain's 1.6 million Muslims are living on a diet of death, hypocrisy and neglect that is traumatising and radicalising an entire generation.'

What does the future hold? Is it indeed the case that an entire generation is being traumatised and radicalised? How can a broadly secular society such as Britain, but with many Christian traditions and reference points, provide space for observant Muslims? How much action has been taken since the alarm was first raised about the debilitating effects of Islamophobia? Has there been a genuine, principled response from officialdom, or just rhetoric and grudging compliance? Why is the antiracist movement so reluctant to address prejudice, hate and discrimination based on religion? Should Islamophobia be defined as a form of racism, in much the same way that antisemitism clearly is, and should the full force of race relations legislation be brought to bear to defeat it? Should a key idea in the Stephen Lawrence Inquiry, institutional racism, be adapted, so that tackling institutional Islamophobia is put firmly on the agenda? Is the failure of the Race Relations (Amendment) Act to refer to anti-Muslim prejudice a poignant example of institutional Islamophobia?

These are the questions explored in this report. The report is about Britain, not the wider world. But events in the wider world affect what happens in Britain. And UK foreign policy, most obviously on the Palestine/Israel situation, has a key influence on the climate of opinion within Britain.

One requirement is for far more face-to-face contact between different communities within Britain. In 2003, in this respect, the Uniting Britain Trust and Alif-Aleph organised a mapping exercise that led to the publication of a report entitled *Positive Contacts between British Muslims and British Jews: a model of good practice for all British communities*. The report outlined four different kinds of contact: (a) pragmatic, for example in relation to regeneration and neighbourhood renewal; (b) political, for example with regard to Israel/Palestine; (c) theological, namely about similarities and differences between the two religions; (d) ethnic/cultural, looking at shared ethnic and cultural practices.

My time with the Stephen Lawrence Inquiry left me in no doubt, however, that personal contacts and personal attitude change are not enough. Robust attention must also be directed at society's institutions and public services, and at their cultures, their corporate 'common sense', and their ways of talking, thinking and working.

All human beings connect most easily to PLUs – People Like Us. But any institution that is controlled by PLUs is likely to be biased, both internally and in its dealings with the outside world. It will benefit PLUs and operate against the interests of, as the term might be, PLTs – People Like Them.

Most major British institutions are led by white, middle-class men – like me. So they have a distinctive responsibility to help make Britain a safer, more inclusive society for all who live here. Racism is not in the minds of black people, nor is Islamophobia in the minds of Muslims, nor antisemitism in the minds of Jews. Racism, Islamophobia and antisemitism are in the minds of white people, non-Muslims and non-Jews, and in the institutions, organisations and cultures that they mould and lead.

Those who are subject to discrimination have crucial roles to play in identifying how discrimination takes place and in articulating the harm it does. But they cannot on their own prevent it from taking place. There has also to be determined action among those who have power and influence.

This report is addressed primarily, therefore, to non-Muslims. I passionately hope that it will be considered and studied in a wide range of forums – committee rooms and council chambers, certainly, but also schools, the media, faith communities, employers and unions – and, even more importantly, that it will be acted on.

Richard Stone is chair of the Commission on British Muslims and Islamophobia.

The quotations in this foreword are from an article by Fuad Nahdi in The Guardian, *1 April 2003.*

The report published by Alif-Aleph UK and the Uniting Britain Trust on Muslim/Jewish contacts was written by Fiona Hurst and Mohammed Nisar supervised by Dr Keith Kahn-Harris.

Copies are available from the Uniting Britain Trust, Barkat House, 116 Finchley Road, London NW3 5HT.

1. TAKING STOCK
Progress, unfinished business and new challenges

Two developments

Two developments since 1997 warrant immediate attention: (a) the work of Muslim organisations and (b) measures taken by government.

The best-known and most representative Muslim umbrella organisation, the Muslim Council of Britain, was established in autumn 1997. It was planned to be similar in its purposes and activities to the Board of Deputies of British Jews and has become the principal channel through which representations by British Muslims are made to central government and to the media.

Other national organisations include Al-Khoei Foundation, An-Nisa Society, British Muslim Research Centre, Forum Against Islamophobia and Racism, Islamic Foundation, Islamic Human Rights Commission, Islamic Society of Britain, IQRA Trust, Ismaili Centre, Muslim Association of Britain and Muslim Parliament. There are in addition several hundred organisations working regionally and nationally, of which the largest include Bradford Council of Mosques and Lancashire Council of Mosques. There are also several substantial Muslim websites. Journals and periodicals with national circulations include *Emel, Impact International, Muslim News, Muslim Weekly* and *Q News.* Further, several organisations send out regular email newsletters and bulletins to their members and contacts, and there are many local and regional bulletins.

The addresses of all the organisations, websites and periodicals mentioned above are given in Appendix C.

Much of the credit for combating and reducing Islamophobia in Britain over the last few years must go to Muslim organisations, working nationally, regionally and locally. But some credit must go to the government also. Notable developments introduced by the government include changes in employment law, so that Muslims are now protected from direct and indirect discrimination in recruitment and workplace practices; changes in the criminal justice system, so that crimes against Muslims attract higher sentences if they are aggravated by anti-Muslim hostility; the appointment of Muslims to chaplaincy roles in hospitals and prisons; the creation of Muslim schools within the state education system; encouragement of inter-faith activity and cooperation, and the involvement of faith communities in neighbourhood renewal; the potential of the community cohesion agenda to promote equality and dialogue in local settings; and greater sensitivity to the concerns and needs of Muslims throughout public services. It is relevant also to mention changes in the financial services industry to accommodate Muslim beliefs and values relating to loans, and increased sensitivity to the dangers of Islamophobia in the media.

In December 2003 a government minister outlined the public philosophy underlying such developments. An extract from her speech is given in Box 1.[1] Positive developments reflecting this philosophy are outlined in Box 2.

Box 1

British, Muslim and proud
A statement of philosophy

In Britain we have a proud tradition of supporting free speech and allowing people to follow their own beliefs. The British way is to support religious freedom. It is tolerant and adaptable. Britishness today is not homogeneous. It is evolving and is as rich as the different people in Britain. British Muslims have consistently shown how it is possible to be British, Muslim and proud.

Throughout the country, Muslims, with their strong commitment to community development, and with enterprise and dedication, are playing a vital role in building a strong and vibrant society.

There has been a long running controversy in France both within the state education system and nationally about symbols and the role of faith in a secular society. This is a debate we had a long time ago, and with our very different traditions and with sensitivity displayed by all faiths, we have been able to find within our own culture a way of celebrating diversity without controversy. For example, a British woman can wear the hijab comfortably in public or in a school. That diversity is something that as a Government we value and why we are developing work on inter-faith dialogue and the importance of understanding of each other's cultures and respect for one another's traditions and values.

Speech by Home Office minister Fiona Mactaggart, December 2003

Box 2

Recognising progress
Important developments, 2001-2003

Discrimination in employment
Since December 2003 it has been unlawful to discriminate on grounds of religion or belief in recruitment and workplace organisation.

Guidance for employers
In autumn 2003 the Advisory, Conciliation and Arbitration Service (ACAS) prepared draft guidance for employers on the operation of the new regulations against religious discrimination that would come into effect in December.

A single equality commission
In October 2003 the government announced, after thorough consultation, that it proposed to merge the three existing equality commissions (for race, gender and disability); to include tackling religious discrimination in the new commission's responsibilities; and to make the commission responsible for human rights issues more generally.

Religiously aggravated crimes
All offences shown to be aggravated by religious hostility attract higher sentences. The Crown Prosecution Service published a formal policy statement on racist and religious crime on 14 July 2003. Attorney General Lord Goldsmith QC, speaking at the launch of the policy, stressed that 'a racially or religiously motivated attack is an attack on the whole community. This policy sends a clear message to perpetrators that they will not get away with threatening, violent or abusive behaviour.' There is fuller information at www.cps.gov.uk

Registration of marriages
The General Register Office published a consultation document *Civil Registration: delivering vital change* in July 2003. It can be read at www.statistics.gov.uj/registration. The overall purpose is to introduce greater equality between different religions and denominations.

New unit at the Home Office
In summer 2003 a new Faith Communities Unit was set up within the Home Office. It took over work on religious issues previously undertaken by staff in the Race Equality Unit (REU) and was situated within a new directorate alongside the REU and the Community Cohesion Unit. It is responsible for faith issues including advising ministers on visits to faith communities; review of government contacts with faith communities; promoting interfaith dialogue; engaging with British Muslims; religious discrimination; racial and religious related hate crime; and policy advice on issues surrounding new religious movements. It is also responsible for Holocaust Memorial Day.

Dress codes
Several police services, following an example set by the Metropolitan Police, have adjusted their dress codes to make them more 'Muslim-friendly'. Similar adjustments have been made by the Ministry of Defence.

Prison Service
In 1999 the post of Muslim Adviser was created in the headquarters chaplaincy team to supervise arrangements for imams to act as 'chaplains' to Muslim prisoners and, more generally, to advise on meeting Muslims' religious and pastoral needs.

Hospitals
Many hospital trusts now employ Muslim 'chaplains' and provide multi-faith prayer rooms for patients and staff.

Department for International Development (DfID)
DfID has produced material about its work overseas that is designed to be of special interest to British Muslims.

Foreign and Commonwealth Office (FCO)
The FCO has set up services to support British Muslims performing the Hajj pilgrimage and, for example, runs a consular office at Mecca at certain times of the year. It works in partnership with the Department of Health in the provision of advice about vaccination requirements. In 2003 the first British Muslim ambassador was appointed.

Disappointment and concern

But it's not all good news. For the compilation of the opening chapter of this report interviews and conversations were held in November 2003 around the topic of 'taking stock'. In what ways have things improved since 1997, and in what ways have they got worse? This was the basic question. Interviewees were invited also to give brief statements in writing, if they wished.

There was acknowledgement in the responses of progress and improvements but also much disappointment, and a sense that in certain respects change has been cosmetic not real. Further, there was recurring reference to the negative effects of 9/11 and the ensuing wars, and of the ways in which the civil liberties of Muslims in Britain have become severely curtailed. Alongside the positive note struck in Boxes 1 and 2 must stand the criticism and disappointment cited in Box 3.

'After Sept 11th,' said Baroness Uddin in one of the interviews, 'the Prime Minister made a real effort to communicate to the world that ordinary Muslims were not the target of the effort to tackle terrorism. But actions spoke louder than words and the attacks on Iraq have taken us back decades. The perception that our Government is pandering to the neo conservatives of America has given rise to the belief that all Muslims are implicated in the aggression. Each of us is constantly being asked to apologise for the acts of terror that befall the world. To make matters worse, there is not a day that we do not have to face comments so ignorant that even Enoch Powell would not have made them.'[2]

Murad Qureshi, a borough councillor, agreed: 'The climate has changed alarmingly in recent years. When you start seeing ministers such as foreign office minister Dennis MacShane targeting Muslims that is a clear indication of just how stark the situation has become.'

Qureshi continued: 'Muslims have become the new political black. But the race relations industry has failed to take that on board. I am very disappointed with the response of the CRE and the Home Office... I went to school in west London with a lot of black lads and I never had the kind of grief that they had from the police. But I am beginning to realise how they felt.'

Box 3

Very little progress

It is the view of the Muslim Council of Britain that very little progress has been made in tackling the horror of Islamophobia in the United Kingdom since it was brought into sharp focus by the Commission on British Muslims and Islamophobia in its report published in 1997.

Whilst we recognise the adverse impact of international politics on the perception of Islam generally and Muslims living in the United Kingdom, we strongly feel that the government has done little to discharge its responsibilities under international law to protect its Muslim citizens and residents from discrimination, vilification, harassment, and deprivation.

The legal framework required to articulate standards of behaviour and to bring about a cohesive society remains as inadequate as it was when the report was published by the Commission in 1997.

Source: statement by the Muslim Council of Britain, November 2003

Sadiq Khan, a senior lawyer and chair of the Muslim Council of Britain's legal affairs committee, similarly commented on race equality legislation. 'Through a process of trickle down,' he said, 'many of the recommendations arising from the Macpherson report have had some benefit for Muslim communities. The extension of the Race Relations Act, for example, is having an indirect positive effect. But opportunities have been missed. The Race Relations Act could have been amended to include religions as well as races. Secondary legislation and regulations were used to bring in laws preventing discrimination on the grounds of religion in employment and occupation. However, the Government could have passed primary legislation, which would have been more effective.'

Khan also spoke about anti-terrorism legislation: 'Criminal laws such as the Terrorism Act 2000 and the Anti-Terrorism Crime Security Act 2001 have helped to create a climate of fear. They have led to the internment in the UK of Muslim men, respectable charities having their funds seized, and charities suffering because Muslims are reluctant to donate money for fear of being accused of funding 'terrorists'.

'It requires a lot of strength,' said Mohammed Umar, a publisher, 'to fight back. But we have the history, religion and cultural background to withstand this. Once Muslims in Britain realise how much this country needs them the more we can start moving forward economically. Young Muslims are talented, energetic kids full of mental and physical resources.' He was confident that things would eventually get better: 'In a strange way, Islamophobia is bringing us together. Muslims have no common language and come from many cultures with their own traditions that have nothing to do with Islam. They will stand side by side in the mosque, but there are divisions. But now we are the common enemy and that is fostering relationships. The Pakistani, the Nigerian, the black convert from Jamaica – we are starting to see each other as brothers.'

Golshad Ghiaci is originally from Iran. She came to Britain in 1967 and is a psychotherapist. I don't know whether Islamophobia has got worse or whether it has just come to the surface since 11 September. 'I certainly wasn't aware of it so much before then. Of course, there has always been prejudice against Arabs, and now I suppose the two are linked. It has become much more blatant. Now Muslims are baddies, we are a bunch of terrorists bent on killing and destroying, we are lunatics and that's what we do – we blow things up. There doesn't seem to be much that's good about us.'

Gone backwards

'Opening a newspaper every day,' Ghiaci continued, 'or turning on the television and seeing the wars in Iraq and Afghanistan, seeing what's happening in Guantanamo Bay and the way the Terrorism Act is being used to just round people up and put them away...it's kind of dehumanising. I feel this overwhelming sense of rage and outrage. It's as though everything that's bad in the world is being projected onto us. I was going crazy for a while after September 11. I think a lot of us did. But I decided a while ago I would have to calm down or I would go mad. It's mindblowing, because nobody seems to mind. Islamophobia is a societal thing and it's as though people aren't aware how bad things are. Muslims are an easy target because we are visibly different. And people always need some focus for their hatred.'

'In terms of Islamophobia, we have gone backwards,' said Rashad Yaqoob, a solicitor. 'All the attempts to improve things over the last five to ten years have been completely dismantled following 9/11. At a government level, British Muslims feel completely ignored and demonised. Blair has probably let down Muslims more than anyone else because we backed him. He has repaid us by reneging on all his promises, and it's a complete betrayal of trust. We have been through an emotional rollercoaster watching our Muslim brothers die. It makes us feel like cannon fodder.'

Government policy on refugees, he said, 'has played directly into the hands of the neo-fascists. They don't differentiate between someone standing in the street with a begging bowl and someone wearing an Armani suit and driving a flash car – in the end you are still a Paki. That's the way it feels. And the vicious new legislation on terrorism has given the police and security services powers they could never have got away with five years ago. I have 50 clients sitting in cells right now for one reason and one reason only: they are Muslim.

Yaqoob ended his statement on a note of anger and near despair: 'I lost a friend on 9/11. We suffered like anybody else suffered but now we are expected to feel guilty for the rest of our lives. The cry from London to Bradford, from Birmingham to Bolton, is injustice, injustice, injustice.'

Energy and defiance

DJ and broadcaster Imran Khan responded to the interview with a short story, shown in Box 4. He imagined the world through the eyes of a 16-year-old youth in Manchester, 'Ash'. For Ash, he comments, Islamophobia is 'just racism with a spin'. Ash is aware that Islamophobia exists in the media, in the education system and in employment. But where it matters, so far as he is concerned, is in the street. It's the street that has to be claimed and defended. Khan's pen-portrait salutes the energy and defiance of the urban young and their determination not to be subdued. It leaves the reader in doubt, though, about the eventual outcomes, and about whether life for Ash and Ash's generation – and for Britain more generally – is getting better or worse.

Box 4

Racism with a spin
Same shit, different lyrics

Manchester 2003. Wilmslow Rd, otherwise known as curry mile. Eid. Just after dark the atmosphere grows ever more expectant, the cars get just that little bit louder, the flags – Pakistani and Palestinian – start to wave with a bit more force. In Bury a riot of colour breaks out in an otherwise grey suburb, beats bang from the stereo. 'Tonight we celebrate', thinks Ash as he steps out the bathroom. Just 16, Ash is razor-sharp cool incarnate. For him Islamophobia is just racism with a spin: 'They used to call me Paki, now they call me Bin Laden fucker, same shit, different lyrics.'

It's a common attitude from many youths Ash's age. Same shit, different lyrics. Tonight on the Wilmslow Road thousands of Ashs will be on the street. They will be in power, loud, out and proud. For Ash's generation Islamophobia isn't in the media, it isn't in the schools or the workplace, it's in the street, in the kickings that are doled out by the white lads to 'mini Bin Ladens' and the disdainful looks, and sometimes worse, that the white girls give to young Muslim girls because they wear hijab.

Tonight, though, the street. The night is Ash's. For one night only Islamophobia, racism, call it what you will, is not on the menu. As Ash hits the street and settles into his purple SR Nova with the 10 inch rims, he thinks: 'They might own the day, right, but tonight this street is pure mine.'

The uncertain note on which Khan's story ends is a fitting start to this report as a whole. It needs to be accompanied, however, by an upbeat vision of the future. Such a vision is sketched below.

Vision for the future

The 1997 report on Islamophobia included a statement of vision. It is reprinted here in Box 5. Together with doubts and fears expressed earlier in this chapter, and with the review of positive developments summarised in Box 2, it provides the context for the report that follows.

Box 5

The day will come
A statement of vision

The day will come when:

1 British Muslims participate fully and confidently at all levels in the political, cultural, social and economic life of the country.

2 The voices of British Muslims are fully heard and held in the same respect as the voices of other communities and groups. Their individual and collective contributions to wider society are acknowledged and celebrated, locally, regionally and nationally.'

3 Islamophobic behaviour is recognised as unacceptable and is no longer be tolerated in public. Whenever it occurs people in positions of leadership and influence speak out and condemn it.

4 Legal sanctions against religious discrimination in employment and service delivery are on the statute book and offences aggravated by religious hostility are dealt with severely.

5 The state system of education includes a number of Muslim schools, and all mainstream state schools provide effectively for the pastoral, religious and cultural needs of their Muslim pupils. The range of academic attainment amongst Muslim pupils and students is the same as for the country generally.

6 The need of young British Muslims to develop their religious and cultural identity in a British context is accepted and supported.

7 Measures to tackle social and economic deprivation, unemployment and neighbourhood renewal are of benefit to Muslims as to all other communities.

8 All employers and service providers ensure that, in addition to compliance with legal requirements on non-discrimination, they demonstrate high regard for religious, cultural and ethnic diversity.

Source: Runnymede Trust Commission on British Muslims and Islamophobia, 1997, slightly adapted

2. ATTITUDES AND INSTITUTIONS
Islamophobia and racism

Summary

This chapter begins with evidence that Islamophobia has been present in western culture for many centuries. It has taken different forms, however, at different times and in different contexts. The chapter discusses the arguments for seeing Islamophobia as a form of racism and observes that most race equality organisations have not yet adequately responded to the challenges that Islamophobia poses. It closes by discussing the concept of 'institutional Islamophobia'.

A new word for an old fear

Hostility towards Islam and Muslims has been a feature of European societies since the eighth century of the common era. It has taken different forms at different times and has fulfilled a variety of functions. For example, the hostility in Spain in the fifteenth century was not the same as the hostility that was expressed and mobilised in the Crusades. Nor was the hostility during the time of the Ottoman Empire or that which prevailed throughout the age of empires and colonialism.[1] It may be more apt to speak of 'Islamophobias' rather than of a single phenomenon. Each version of Islamophobia has its own features as well as similarities with, and borrowings from, other versions.

A key factor since the1960s is the presence of some fifteen million Muslim people in western European countries. Another is the increased economic leverage on the world stage of oil-rich countries, many of which are Muslim in their culture and traditions. A third is the abuse of human rights by repressive regimes that claim to be motivated and justified by Muslim beliefs. A fourth is the emergence of political movements that similarly claim to be motivated by Islam and that use terrorist tactics to achieve their aims.

This report is about Islamophobia directed against Muslims in Britain at the present time, not about world politics or international relations or the situation in other Western countries, and not about the past. But it necessarily refers to the wider context from time to time, both spatially and historically, and is mindful of it throughout. One of its chapters (chapter 3) is specifically about the impact of 9/11 and the ensuing wars in Afghanistan and Iraq, and about the impact of British foreign policy on the perceptions and experience of British Muslims. The bibliography includes works about Islamophobia in other countries as well as Britain, for example publications from the European Monitoring Centre on Racism and Xenophobia, and reports by the United Nations and the US State Department.[2]

Examples

In Britain as in other European countries, manifestations of anti-Muslim hostility include:

- verbal and physical attacks on Muslims in public places[3]

- attacks on mosques and desecration of Muslim cemeteries

- widespread and routine negative stereotypes in the media, including the broadsheets, and in the conversations and 'common sense' of non-Muslims – people talk and write about Muslims in ways that would not be acceptable if the reference were to Jewish people, for example, or to black people

- negative stereotypes and remarks in speeches by political leaders, implying that Muslims in Britain are less committed than others to democracy and the rule of law – for example the claim that Muslims more than others must choose between 'the British way' and 'the terrorist way'[4]

- discrimination in recruitment and employment practices, and in workplace cultures and customs

- bureaucratic delay and inertia in responding to Muslim requests for cultural sensitivity in education and healthcare and in planning applications for mosques

- lack of attention to the fact that Muslims in Britain are disproportionately affected by poverty and social exclusion

- non-recognition of Muslims in particular, and of religion in general, by the law of the land, since discrimination in employment on grounds of religion has until recently been lawful and discrimination in the provision of services is still lawful

- anomalies in public order legislation, such that Muslims are less protected against incitement to hatred than members of certain other religions

- laws curtailing civil liberties that disproportionately affect Muslims.

Several of these matters are discussed in later chapters – poverty and social exclusion in chapter 5, discrimination and employment in chapter 6, hate crime and civil liberties in chapter 7, and the media in chapter 10.

Contextual factors

Islamophobia is exacerbated by a number of contextual factors. One of these is the fact that a high proportion of refugees and people seeking asylum are Muslims. Demonisation of refugees by the tabloid press is therefore frequently a coded attack on Muslims, for the words 'Muslim', 'asylum-seeker', 'refugee' and 'immigrant' become synonymous and interchangeable with each other in the popular imagination. Occasionally, the connection is made entirely explicit. For example, a newspaper recycling the myth that asylum-seekers are typically given luxury space by the government in five-star accommodation added in one recent account that they are supplied also with 'library, gym and even free prayer-mats'.[5] A member of the House of Lords wishing to evoke in a succinct phrase people who are undesirable spoke of '25-year-old black Lesbians and

homosexual Muslim asylum-seekers'.[6] In 2003, when the Home Office produced a poster about alleged deceit and dishonesty amongst people seeking asylum, it chose to illustrate its concerns by focusing on someone with a Muslim name.[7] An end-of-year article in the *Sunday Times* magazine on 'Inhumanity to Man' during 2003 focused in four of its five examples on actions by Muslims.[8]

'We have thousands of asylum seekers from Iran, Iraq, Algeria, Egypt, Libya, Yemen, Saudi Arabia and other Arab countries living happily in this country on social security,' writes a journalist in January 2004. Arabs, he says in the same article, are 'threatening our civilian populations with chemical and biological weapons. They are promising to let suicide bombers loose in Western and American cities. They are trying to terrorise us, disrupt our lives.'[9]

A second contextual factor is the sceptical, secular and agnostic outlook with regard to religion that is reflected implicitly, and sometimes expressed explicitly, in the media, perhaps particularly the left-liberal media.[10] The outlook is opposed to all religion, not to Islam only. Commenting on media treatment of the Church of England, the Archbishop of Canterbury remarked in a speech in summer 2003 that in the eyes of the media the church is a kind of soap opera: 'Its life is about short-term conflicts, blazing rows in the pub, so to speak, mysterious plots and unfathomable motivations. It is both ridiculous and fascinating. As with soap operas, we, the public, know that real people don't actually live like that, but we relish the drama and become fond of the regular cast of unlikely characters with, in this case, their extraordinary titles and bizarre costumes.'[11] At first sight, the ridiculing of religion by the media is even-handed. But the Church of England, for example, has far more resources with which to combat malicious or ignorant media coverage than does British Islam. For Muslims, since they have less influence and less access to public platforms, attacks are far more undermining. Debates and disagreements about religion are legitimate in modern society and indeed are to be welcomed. But they do not take place on a level playing-field.

A third contextual factor is UK foreign policy in relation to various conflict situations around the world. There is a widespread perception that the war on terror is in fact a war on Islam, and that the UK supports Israel against Palestinians. In other conflicts too the UK government appears to side with non Muslims against Muslims and to collude with the view that the terms 'Muslim' and 'terrorist' are synonymous. These perceptions of UK foreign policy may or may not be accurate. The point is that they help fashion the lens through which events inside Britain are interpreted – not only by Muslims but by non-Muslims as well. There is fuller discussion of the international context in chapter 3.

The cumulative effect of Islamophobia's various features, exacerbated by the contextual factors mentioned above, is that Muslims are made to feel that they do not truly belong here – they feel that they are not truly accepted, let alone welcomed, as full members of British society. On the contrary, they are seen as 'an enemy within' or 'a fifth column' and they feel that they are under constant siege.[12] This is bad for society as well as for Muslims themselves. Moreover, time-bombs are being primed that are likely to explode in the future – both Muslim and non-Muslim commentators have pointed out that a young generation of British Muslims is developing that feels increasingly disaffected, alienated and bitter. It's in the interests of non-Muslims as well as Muslims, therefore, that Islamophobia should be rigorously challenged, reduced and dispelled. The time to act is now, not some time in the future.

A further negative consequence of Islamophobia is that Muslim insights on ethical and social issues are not given an adequate hearing and are not seen as positive assets. 'Groups such as Muslims in the West,' writes an observer, 'can be part of transcultural dialogues, domestic and global, that might make our societies live up to their promises of diversity and democracy. Such communities can ... facilitate communication and understanding in these fraught and destabilising times.'[13] But Islamophobia makes this potential all but impossible to realise.

'The most subtle and for Muslims perilous consequence of Islamophobic actions,' a Muslim scholar has observed, 'is the silencing of self-criticism and the slide into defending the indefensible. Muslims decline to be openly critical of fellow Muslims, their ideas, activities and rhetoric in mixed company, lest this be seen as giving aid and comfort to the extensive forces of condemnation. Brotherhood, fellow feeling,

sisterhood are genuine and authentic reflexes of Islam. But Islam is supremely a critical, reasoning and ethical framework... [It] cannot, or rather ought not to, be manipulated into 'my fellow Muslim right or wrong'.'[14] She goes on to remark that Islamophobia provides 'the perfect rationale for modern Muslims to become reactive, addicted to a culture of complaint and blame that serves only to increase the powerlessness, impotence and frustration of being a Muslim.'

Violent language

On 11 September 2001 and the following days there were strong feelings of powerlessness and frustration amongst non-Muslims as well as Muslims. When people feel powerless and frustrated they are prone to hit out with violent language. Box 6, for example, shows the kind of violent language that was used in email messages to the Muslim Council of Britain immediately following 9/11. At least one of the writers later apologised. Their messages were nevertheless significant, for they expressed attitudes and imaginings that are widespread amongst non-Muslims, and that are recurring components of Islamophobia.

The term 'Islamophobia' is not, admittedly, ideal, for it implies that one is merely talking about some sort of mental sickness or aberration. Some of the people quoted in Box 6 do indeed sound as if they are mentally unstable. But the imagery, stereotypes and assumptions in their messages are widespread in western countries and are not systematically challenged by influential leaders. The writers quoted in Box 7, for example, are widely respected and are read with approval by millions of people. They don't use obscene language and do observe elementary conventions of spelling, punctuation and grammar. They don't propose violent removal or repatriation of Muslims; don't deploy terms such as 'subhuman freaks', 'animals', 'not people', 'vile' and 'evil'; and don't express pleasure at the thought of Muslim men, women and children being slaughtered. But their basic message, at least in the perception of many British Muslims, seems similar to the one that underlies the inarticulate rants in Box 6 – 'you don't belong here'.

Box 6

You don't belong here

Email messages to the Muslim Council of Britain, September 2001 – March 2003

You don't belong here and you never will. Go back to fornicating with your camels in the desert, and leave us alone. (11/9/01)

Are you happy now? Salman Rushdie was right, your religion is a joke. Long live Israel! The US will soon kill many Muslim women and children. You are all subhuman freaks! (11/9/01).

I really have tried not to follow my father who was a simple racist. However, I saw your people celebrating in Palastine and Libya and I was sick with despair. How on God's earth can you justify killing in this way? HOW can you celebrate? I no longer have any respect for you. None at all. I am so sorry, but I just despise you and your cruel God. You are not people. Just cold killers. May God forgive you but from now on, may the Americans find you and remove you from my country. I can no longer be civil to you. I am so angry, so hurt, just...oh, leave it, leave it there. Just get out of the UK. Go back to your homes and leave us alone. Cowards. (11/9/01).

Have you heard the saying 'crocodile tears', well in my opinion your sentiments of sympathy regarding the attacks in New York and Washington are exactly that. I have never considered myself to be a racist – but I am now...Your kind nows nothing but force .... well you've sown the seed, now reap the whirlwind, you have woken us up to what you all stand for. (12.9.01)

It sickens me to know what a VILE EVIL race you load of Muslims are you have demonstrated this with the destruction in the USA. Get out of my country now! England is for white civilised English people. (12.9.01)

The rest of the world will now join to smash the filthy disease infested Islam you must be removed from Britain in body bags (12.9.01)

hope you like the bombs, payback for your satanic religion. we will kill you all if we have too stay in the stoneage and may islam burn under US bombs. (14/9/01)

Why do you bother to live here? you hate the english with a passion. you hate christianity. you hate america. but all of you like taking our hospitality and money and then turning on us. If we get attacked in this country i along with thousands of normal christians will make absolutely sure that all muslims will suffer. the worst thing this country did was offer refuge to animals who call themselves humans bombing places like the world trade centre is the action of scum. (13/2/03)

We know where to find you. (14/2/03)

Source: this is just a small selection of such messages posted on the website of the Muslim Council of Britain (www.mcb.org.uk). Original spellings and punctuation have been retained.

Opinion in the United States

Remarks and observations such as those quoted in Box 7 have also been made widely in the United States, and it is American writers such as Bernard Lewis and Samuel Huntington who have developed the thesis that there is an irreconcilable clash between Islam and 'the West'.[15] 'The underlying problem for the West,' writes Huntington, 'is not Islamic fundamentalism. It is Islam, a different civilisation whose people are convinced of the superiority of their culture and are obsessed with the inferiority of their power.'[16] Since the climate of opinion in the US has a substantial impact, both direct and indirect, on mindsets and outlooks in Europe, it is important that Europeans should be aware of how it is articulated and

moulded.[17] Box 7 contains a range of quotations from the US in the aftermath of 9/11. Such statements are significant in Britain not only because they affect the climate of opinion here. Also, British Muslims take note of the response or non-response to them by political and church leaders.[18]

Islamophobia and race relations

One of the messages quoted in Box 6 refers to Muslims as a race.[19] In other ways too the language in Boxes 4, 5 and 6 about Islam and Muslims is reminiscent of racism. For example, there is the stereotype that 'they're all the same' – no recognition of debate, disagreement and variety amongst those

Box 7

We have reason to be suspicious
Some columnists' views

Noose
Was world communism ever such a threat as militant Islam now is? If Islam were to draw a noose about the world, could it be resisted, would its political and economic consequences be worse, would its dominion last longer than the half-century of communism after the Iron Curtain dropped?'
Brian Sewell, Evening Standard

Oppressive darkness
Call me a filthy racist – go on, you know you want to – but we have reason to be suspicious of Islam and treat it differently from the other major religions ... While the history of the other religions is one of moving forward out of oppressive darkness and into tolerance, Islam is doing it the other way round.
Julie Birchill, The Guardian

Treachery and deceit
Orientals... shrink from pitched battle, which they often deride as a sort of game, preferring ambush, surprise, treachery and deceit as the best way to overcome an enemy... This war [in Afghanistan] belongs within the much larger spectrum of a far wider conflict between settled, creative, productive Westerners and predatory, destructive Orientals.
John Keegan, The Daily Telegraph, 8 October 2001

Blind, cruel faith
Islamist militancy is a self-confessed threat to the values not merely of the US but also of the European Enlightenment: to the preference for life over death, to peace, rationality, science and the humane treatment of our fellow men, not to mention fellow women. It is a reassertion of blind, cruel faith over reason.
Samuel Brittan, The Financial Times, 31 July 2002

Fifth column
We have a fifth column in our midst... Thousands of alienated young Muslims, most of them born and bred here but who regard themselves as an army within, are waiting for an opportunity to help to destroy the society that sustains them. We now stare into the abyss, aghast.
Melanie Phillips, Sunday Times, 4 November 2001

who are targeted. There is the imagery, also, of 'them' being totally different from 'us' – no sense of shared humanity, or of shared values and aspirations, or of us and them being interdependent and mutually influencing. Indeed, they are so different that they are evil, wicked, cruel, irrational, disloyal, devious and uncivilised. In short, they do not belong here and should be removed. These strongly negative views of the other are accompanied by totally positive views of the self. 'We' are everything that 'they' are not – good, wise, kind, reasonable, loyal, honest and civilised.[20]

It is sometimes suggested, in view of the kinds of stereotype illustrated in Boxes 6, 7, and 8, that a more appropriate term than Islamophobia is 'anti-Muslim racism'.[21] An obvious objection to this suggestion is that Muslims are not a race. However, there is only one race, the human race, and there is an important sense in which black, Asian and Chinese people are not races either. In any case, race relations legislation in Britain refers not only to so-called race but also to nationality and national origins, and to the four nations that comprise the United Kingdom. Further, the legal definition of another key category in the legislation, that of ethnic group, makes no reference to physical appearance and is wide enough to be a definition of religion – if, that is, religion is seen as to do with affiliation and community background rather than, essentially, with beliefs. There is further discussion of this distinction in chapter 5.

The United Nations World Conference Against Racism (WCAR) in 2001 summarised its concerns with the phrase 'racism, racial discrimination,

---

Box 8

A very evil, wicked religion

Islam is, quite simply, a religion of war...
[American Muslims] should be encouraged to
leave. They are a fifth column in this country.
*Why Islam is a Threat to America and the West by
Paul Weyrich and William Lind*

We should invade their countries, kill their leaders
and convert them to Christianity. We weren't
punctilious about locating and punishing only
Hitler and his top officials. We carpet bombed
German cities, and killed civilians. That's war. And
this is war.
*Columnist Ann Coulter, National Review, 13
September 2001*

Muslims pray to a different God ...Islam is a very
evil and wicked religion ...
*Franklin Graham (son of Billy Graham), speech on
NBC Nightly News, November 2001*

They want to coexist until they can control,
dominate and then, if need be, destroy ... I think
Osama bin Laden is probably a very dedicated
follower of Muhammad. He's done exactly what
Muhammad said to do, and we disagree with him
obviously, and I'm sure many moderate Muslims
do as well, but you can't say the Muslim religion is
a religion of peace. It's not.
*Rev Pat Robertson, founder of Christian Coalition,
CNN, February 2002*

Islam is a religion in which God requires you to
send your son to die for him. Christianity is a faith
in which God sends his son to die for you.
*John Ashcroft (US Attorney General), Los Angeles
Times, 16 February 2002*

xenophobia and related intolerance'. The equivalent phrase used by the Council of Europe is 'racism, xenophobia, antisemitism and intolerance'. Both phrases are cumbersome, but valuably signal that there is a complex cluster of matters to be addressed; the single word 'racism', as customarily used, does not encompass them all. In effect the WCAR argued that the term racism should be expanded to refer to a wide range of intolerance, not just to intolerance where the principal marker of difference is physical appearance and skin colour. For example, the term should encompass patterns of prejudice and discrimination such as antisemitism and sectarianism, where the

markers of supposed difference are religious and cultural rather than to do with physical appearance. It is widely acknowledged that antisemitism is a form of racism and in Northern Ireland sectarianism is sometimes referred to as a form of racism.[22] There are clear similarities between antisemitism, sectarianism and Islamophobia, and between these and other forms of intolerance. The plural term 'racisms' is sometimes used to evoke this point.[23]

A description of sectarianism developed by the Corrymeela Community in Northern Ireland is a helpful description of Islamophobia as well:

> Sectarianism is a complex of attitudes, actions, beliefs and structures, at personal, communal and institutional levels ... It arises as a distorted expression of positive human needs, especially for belonging, identity and free expression of difference but is expressed in destructive patterns of relating: hardening the boundaries between groups; overlooking others; belittling, dehumanising or demonising others; justifying or collaborating in the domination of others; physically intimidating or attacking others.[24]

But in addition to similarities with other forms of intolerance and racism, Islamophobia has its own specific features. Action against it must therefore be explicit and focused – it cannot be left to chance within larger campaigns. Unfortunately, race equality organisations in Britain have been slow to recognise Islamophobia as something they ought to deal with. Already in the 1980s there were campaigns at local levels – one of the most sustained and influential was mobilised by the An-Nisa Society in north west London – to persuade race equality organisations to take action against anti-Muslim hostility and discrimination. The concern was in particular with discrimination and insensitivity in the provision of public services, and with the failure of race relations legislation to prevent such discrimination.[25]

Major representations were made by Muslims during the review of race relations legislation that took place in the early 1990s.[26] The categories in race relations legislation, it was pointed out, derived from the colonial period, when Europeans made a simple distinction between themselves and 'lesser breeds', and when the principal marker of difference was skin colour. In Britain, not-white people were divided into two broad categories, 'black' and 'Asian'. Little or no account was made, in this colonial categorisation, of people's inner feelings, self-understandings, narratives, perceptions, ethics, spirituality or religious beliefs. Nor, it follows, was account taken of the moral resources on which people drew to resist discrimination and prejudice against them. Continual use of the category 'Asian' by the race relations industry, to refer to most not-white people who were not categorised as black, meant that Muslims were rendered invisible. Even local authorities which in other respects were at the forefront of implementing race equality legislation, for example Brent, subsumed Muslims under the blanket category of 'Asians'. They were insensitive and unresponsive, in consequence, to distinctive Muslim concerns. A third of all British Muslims are not Asians and a half of all Asians are not Muslims. The insensitivity was – and is – particularly serious in relation to the provision and delivery of services. There is further discussion of service delivery issues in chapter 7.

The objections made by organisations such as An-Nisa in the 1980s and early 90s were ignored by the government. So was a series of articles and editorials throughout the 1990s in the Muslim magazine *Q News*.[27] At the end of the decade, when the Stephen Lawrence Inquiry report was published, an article in *Q News* by a director of the An-Nisa Society observed that race equality legislation had 'reduced the Muslims, the largest minority in Britain, to a deprived and disadvantaged community, almost in a state of siege ... Much as Muslims want to confront racism, they have become disillusioned with an antiracism movement that refuses to combat Islamophobia and which, in many instances, is as oppressive as the establishment itself.'[28] A follow-up article declared that 'the Muslim community has little faith left in the race industry, at the helm of which is the CRE' and spoke of the CRE's 'mean-spirited hostility' towards Muslims.[29]

Back in 1975/76, when the Race Relations Act was being drafted and agreed, there was discussion in parliament at committee stage about whether to include religion, along with nationality and ethnicity, in the legislation.[30] The argument was made particularly by Conservative members, supported by some Labour members. The committee as a whole, however, decided to leave religion out, since at that time discrimination on grounds of religion was not considered to be a major harm that had to be addressed. Twenty-five years later, when the Act was amended, the discussion was renewed.[31] But again the government decided not to include religion. Further, no explicit reference to religion appeared in the various codes of practice about the amended legislation issued by the Commission for Racial Equality. There is further discussion of anti-discrimination legislation in chapter 7.

Meanwhile it is relevant to note that since December 2003, due to legislative requirements at European level rather than to a principled decision by the UK government, discrimination on grounds of religion or belief in employment has been unlawful. For rather longer there has been an anomaly, due to developments in case law since 1976, whereby Jews and Sikhs are defined as ethnic groups and are therefore protected by race relations legislation. The anomaly has been a standing insult to Muslims for two decades and was only partly removed in December 2003. It is still the case that anti-Muslim discrimination is permitted in the provision of goods and services, and in the regulatory functions of public bodies. Public bodies have a positive duty to promote race equality but are not even encouraged, let alone required, to give explicit attention to religion.

Institutional Islamophobia

The failure of race equality organisations and activists over many years to include Islamophobia in their programmes and campaigns appears to be an example of institutional discrimination.

'The concept of institutional racism,' said the Stephen Lawrence Inquiry report, '... is generally accepted, even if a long trawl through the work of academics and activists produces varied words and phrases in pursuit of a definition.' The report cited several of the submissions that it had received during its deliberations and included a definition of its own. If the term 'racism' is replaced by the term 'Islamophobia' in the statements and submissions, and if other changes or additions are made as appropriate, the definitions are as shown in Box 9.[32]

Box 9

Institutional Islamophobia
Notes towards a definition

Reflecting and producing inequalities

Institutional Islamophobia may be defined as those established laws, customs and practices which systematically reflect and produce inequalities in society between Muslims and non-Muslims. If such inequalities accrue to institutional laws, customs or practices, an institution is Islamophobic whether or not the individuals maintaining those practices have Islamophobic intentions. (Adapted from a statement by the Commission for Racial Equality.)

Inbuilt pervasiveness

Differential treatment need be neither conscious nor intentional, and it may be practised routinely by officers whose professionalism is exemplary in all other respects. There is great danger that focusing on overt acts of personal Islamophobia by individual officers may deflect attention from the much greater institutional challenge ... of addressing the more subtle and concealed form that organisational-level Islamophobia may take. Its most important challenging feature is its predominantly hidden character and its inbuilt pervasiveness within the occupational culture. (Adapted from a statement by Dr Robin Oakley)

Collective failure

The collective failure of an organisation to provide an appropriate and professional service to Muslims because of their religion. It can be seen or detected in processes, attitudes and behaviour which amount to discrimination through unwitting prejudice, ignorance, thoughtlessness and stereotyping which disadvantage Muslims. (Adapted from the Stephen Lawrence Inquiry report.)

Culture, customs and routines

The concept refers to systemic disadvantage and inequality in society as a whole and to attitudes, behaviours and assumptions in the culture, customs and routines of an organisation whose consequences are that (a) Muslim individuals and communities do not receive an appropriate professional service from the organisation (b) Muslim staff are insufficiently involved in the organisation's management and leadership and (c) patterns of inequality in wider society between Muslims and non-Muslims are perpetuated not challenged and altered. (Adapted from a statement by the Churches' Commission for Racial Justice.)

3. THE INTERNATIONAL CONTEXT
The impact of 9/11 and war

Summary

Opinions and events in Britain are inevitably affected by opinions and events elsewhere and by Britain's engagements with other countries. This chapter discusses the ways in which Islam was demonised in the media after the attacks in New York and Washington on 11 September 2001, and during the ensuing wars. It closes by quoting several statements that call, explicitly or implicitly, for 'a great conversation'.

The enemy as demon

Always at times of international conflict and fear there is a tendency in the media and in political speeches, and in everyday conversations up and down the land, to dehumanise and demonise the enemy. Simultaneously, there is a tendency to idealise one's own side, with the result that the world becomes comfortingly simplified into two camps, bad guys (them) and good guys (us). The enemy is portrayed as implacably opposed to us and to all we stand for; as evil and barbaric; and as deserving of punishment, suppression and even death. Also, the enemy is less intelligent and rational than we are, has a poorer sense of proportion and cannot be argued with. The only language the enemy understands is force. Casualties inflicted on the enemy are less serious ethically or legally than casualties suffered by one's own side.

Demonising the enemy always involves paying attention to, and laying great stress on, any characteristics that mark out differences between the enemy and one's own side. For example, differences to do with language, dress, food, customs, history, clothing, landscape, facial features – and, crucially, religion. The more obviously different 'they' can be pictured as from 'us', the easier it is to justify hostility towards them and to mobilise support for military action against them. If they have a different religion from us it's as if they inhabit a different planet – a different earth, a different heaven, a different hell. And it's all the easier to believe that the gods are on our side, and not at all on theirs. It has been said that truth is the first casualty in times of war: yes, and God is

the first conscript. A divine seal of approval is invaluable for mobilising support and obedience, quietening uneasy consciences and maintaining morale.

'Historically,' the Archbishop of Canterbury said in his Christmas Day sermon in 2003, 'religious faith has too often been the language of the powerful, the excuse for oppression, the alibi for atrocity. It has appeared as itself intolerant of difference (hence the legacy of antisemitism), as a campaigning, aggressive force for uniformity, as a self-defensive and often corrupt set of institutions indifferent to basic human welfare. That's a legacy that dies hard, however much we might want to protest that it is far from the whole picture. And it's given new life by the threat of terror carried out in the name of a religion – even when representatives of that religion at every level roundly condemn such action as incompatible with faith.'[1]

In Box 8 in the previous chapter ('A very evil, wicked religion') there were examples of how Christianity has been conscripted into present global struggles. Similar examples could be readily cited with regard to Islam. Processes of demonisation and claiming divine justification are certainly not one-way. This report is about Islamophobia, not about – as the term sometimes is – 'westophobia'. However, there are several references to the dangers of westophobia and to the need for Muslims and non-Muslims to work together on combating both kinds of intolerance, particularly when intolerance claims to have religious justification.[2]

'Cannot be held at bay with words'

After 9/11 and during the wars in Afghanistan and Iraq, responsible politicians and newspaper editors maintained that the war on terror was not a war on Islam. Box 10 shows a selection of headlines from the *Sun* and *Mirror* newspapers about this. Politicians and editors emphasised that the vast majority of Muslims are peaceful and law-abiding, and that Muslims who claim a religious justification for terrorism are a tiny unrepresentative minority.

Haleh Afshar, professor of politics and women's studies at the University of York, recalls that she was in a taxi in Birmingham on 11 September 2001, listening to the news:

> When the driver realised I was a Muslim he slowed down to a walking speed. He wanted to know what we as Muslims as a whole could do and what he as a Muslim in Birmingham should do. As an older woman and a Muslim I was expected to help, to tell him how to cope with the avalanche that he assured me was about to descend. Academics are cocooned in the security of the ivory tower – I felt I could assure him that the British were sane, they were not prejudiced. We were both assured by the arrival of the Prime Minister on the airwaves telling the British it was not the Muslims as a whole that were to blame, but a specific group. So he delivered me to the station and we were both relatively reassured by the Prime Minister's speech.

'But,' she continues sorrowfully, 'Islamophobia cannot be held at bay by words.' She describes a casual remark a few days later by a young student at her university. The remark, made in her office at her university – 'that very ivory tower that is supposed to protect us' – indicated in passing that the student didn't even begin to see her as a fellow-citizen of the United Kingdom:

> It is the unexpectedness of Islamophobia and its virulence in the calmest of surroundings that is shocking. The ascribed identity is thrown at you as if it were a reality, as if the marks of years of education, boarding school, elocution classes and a lifetime of living and working in Britain have never diminished the foreignness that I was born with, forever the outsider.

Box 10

Don't blame the Muslims
Headlines in September 2001

Islam is not Evil Religion: the whole world lines up to condemn murderous fanatics
The Sun, 13 September

Don't Blame the Muslims
The Mirror, 14 September

Reach Out to Muslims as Friends
The Sun, 17 September

We Know the Vast Majority of Muslims Condemn Atrocities
Article by the Prime Minister, Sunday People, 23 September

One Britain, Standing Up to Terrorism – to believe that all Muslims should be blamed for those appalling crimes is both ignorant and disgusting
The Mirror, 28 September

Don't Blame Islam for the Madness of Terrorists
Sunday Mirror, 30 September

Thousands of other British Muslims have similar tales to tell from the days after 9/11 – rudeness and insensitivity, or worse, from colleagues, associates and neighbours, and from total strangers in shops and on buses, trains and streets. 'Bigoted white Britons of all social classes,' observed a Muslim journalist bitterly in November 2001, 'now think they have right on their side and so they crush and demean Asian Britons, because brown-skinned people are all damned Pakis who support terrorism that kills their sweet American brothers and sisters.'[3]

One reason why Islamophobia cannot be held at bay with words is that it resides in, and is communicated through, stories and imagery. It is relevant, therefore, to consider the imagery in political cartoons in the British press in autumn 2001. A French academic, Pascale Villate-Compton at the University of Tours, examined this in depth. The account below draws extensively on his research and reflections.

'This means war – with abroad'

Politicians and other influence leaders wanted to avoid demonising Islam after 9/11, they maintained (see

Box 5), but they did wish to contend that terrorists were totally opposed to all things Western. 'The perpetrators acted out of hatred for the values cherished in the West such as freedom, tolerance, prosperity, religious pluralism and universal suffrage,' declared the *New York Times* (16 September). The American President spoke of 'a monumental struggle of Good versus Evil'. The influential writer Francis Fukuyama wrote in *Newsweek*: 'Mohammed Atta and several of the hijackers were educated people who lived and studied in the West. Not only were they not seduced by it, they were sufficiently repelled by what they saw to be willing to drive planes into buildings and kill thousands of people among whom they lived.' A columnist in Britain declared of Osama bin Laden: 'He has a pathological hatred of the West and wants it to be permanently harmed.'[4]

One of the first comments by a political cartoonist after 9/11 was from Steve Bell in *The Guardian*. His picture appeared on 13 September. It showed President Bush announcing: 'This means war...' and Tony Blair adding, by way of clarification: '...with abroad.' It was a comment on the new international situation in which the word 'war' now has to be used. The combatants are not necessarily, any longer, nation states, but much more amorphous and difficult to identify and deal with.[5] The cartoonist was also poking fun at leaders whose bid for military leadership is unaccompanied by precision about who exactly the enemy is. The concept of 'abroad' is, to put it mildly, unfocused. Bell portrayed the American president as Darth Vader, the character in *Star Wars* who personifies anti-Western evil. The real enemies of the West, the cartoonist appeared to be saying, are leaders who unfocusedly demonise 'abroad', and the many millions of people who accept such leadership.

The cartoonist was also, consciously or otherwise, depicting a professional problem that he himself had to contend with. If the enemy is unfocused – if, indeed, the enemy has neither face not form – how can cartoonists depict him or her? Or it or them? Exercise of the political cartoonist's trade is all but impossible without a widely shared stock of readily recognised images, faces and symbols. In cartoons, one recognises Frenchmen by their berets, socialists by their beards, burglars by their striped shirts, vicars by their dog collars, civil servants by their rolled

umbrellas, teachers by their academic gowns, intellectuals by their spectacles, capitalists by their top hats. But there are no stock images for 'abroad'.

This problem for cartoonists was quickly solved. The enemy, they agreed, was a man with an unkempt beard, a turban, flowing robes, a Kalashnikov rifle, an enigmatic smile and a large hooked nose. In so far as there was real person with these features, or widely believed to have these features, it was Osama Bin Laden. In the iconography and stock images of cartoonists post-9/11, however, the reference was rather wider – the enemy was not an individual human being, nor the organisation of which he was the figurehead, nor the strands within Islam known as Islamism, but the whole of Islam. In addition to beards, turbans and loose clothing, and to long, hooked noses, bin Laden and his followers were associated with recurring images of what the Western imagination supposes to be quintessential Islam. Examples included magical flying carpets, with their implications of exotic and alluring irrationality; genies kept in bottles and lamps, evoking dark, destructive, uncontrollable forces; scimitar-shaped swords, symbolising primitive cruelty; and minarets, implying foreign, outlandish beliefs and practices. This was how, in the weeks following 9/11, 'abroad' was pictured and conceptualised. Box 11 describes just a handful of the many political cartoons in the British press (there were well over 100 altogether) about 9/11 and Afghanistan in autumn 2001.

The examples in Box 11 indicate that the enemy was frequently portrayed as evil and profoundly threatening. Also, a recurring emphasis was that he was stupid, naïve, unsophisticated, unscientific, primitive, a figure of fun. But whether evil or stupid or both, the subliminal message was always that 'we' (we newspaper readers in 'the West') are different from 'them'. We are good not evil and are civilised not crude. And – a point made by all cartoons by their very nature – we have a sense of proportion and a GSOH, a good sense of humour.

Neo-conservatism

In an article entitled 'Islamism is the new bolshevism' in the *New York Times* in early 2002, Margaret Thatcher succinctly sketched out the neo-conservative view of priorities in American foreign policy.[6] The

Box 11

The world's nightmare
– cartoons in the British press, autumn 2001

Muslims of the world unite
Bin Laden is depicted as a spider inviting every Muslim in the world to join his network. The words 'Muslims of the world unite' (echoing the Communist Manifesto) are woven into the web. 'Won't you come into my parlour', runs the caption, 'said the spider to the fly.' *Daily Telegraph* 11.10.01.

World in ruins
Bin Laden's Islamic turban and beard mutate into a mushroom cloud hovering over a world in ruins. 'One man's dream,' says the caption, 'the world's nightmare.' *The Times*, 29.9.01

Clones
In his cave in Afghanistan, Bin Laden is shown creating clones of himself in test-tubes, each complete with turban, beard, big nose and enigmatic facial expression. *Daily Express*, 27.11.01

Depravity
Bin Laden has destroyed New York and has replaced the Statue of Liberty with a statue of himself. He holds a bomb in one hand and in the other, instead of a torch, a tablet of stone with words dictated by Allah, entitled *Terrorism*. The word *Liberty* has been removed and thrown into the water, and replaced by *Depravity*. *Daily Mail*, 13.0.01

Give it time
A triptych shows Yasser Arafat, Gerry Adams and Osama bin Laden. They have facial features in common (particularly their big noses). The first two, it is said, have changed from being BAD to being GOOD. Bin Laden is still BAD but he smiles confidently and says 'Give it time'. One day, the implication is, he will destroy the West by holding sway within the West's own heart and mind. *The Times*, 16.10.01

Feeding off the host
British Muslims are shown all dressed like bin Laden and engaged in a demonstration near the Houses of Parliament. 'Death to America,' says one of the placards. The caption indicates that the demonstrators are parasites and explains with a dictionary quotation what this means: '... feeding off the host ... providing no benefit'. *Daily Mail*, 20.9.01

Feeding the cat
A white British housewife talks over the garden fence to her Muslim nextdoor neighbour, the latter clad today in an all-enveloping burka. 'Will you feed the cat for me?' asks the Muslim. 'I'm off to Afghanistan to fight for the Taliban.' *Daily Express*, 31.10.01

article is worth quoting at some length, in order to recall the world-view that holds sway not only in the United States but also amongst the US administration's supporters elsewhere:

> America will never be the same again. It has proved to itself and to others that it is in truth (not just in name) the only global superpower, indeed a power that enjoys a level of superiority over its actual or potential rivals unmatched by any other nation in modern times... As long as America works to maintain its technological lead, there is no reason why any challenge to American dominance should succeed. And that in turn will help ensure stability and peace.

> Yet, as President Bush has reminded Americans, there is no room for complacency. America and its allies, indeed the western world and its values, are still under deadly threat. That threat must be eliminated, and now is the time to act vigorously.

In many respects the challenge of Islamic terror is unique, hence the difficulty western intelligence services encountered trying to predict and prevent its onslaughts. The enemy is not, of course, a religion – most Muslims deplore what has occurred. Nor is it a single state, though this form of terrorism needs the support of states to give it succour. Perhaps the best parallel is with early communism. Islamic extremism today, like bolshevism in the past, is an armed doctrine. It is an aggressive ideology promoted by fanatical, well-armed devotees. And, like communism, it requires an all-embracing long-term strategy to defeat it.

The article then proclaimed that the United States should strike at 'centres of Islamic terror that have taken root in Africa, Southeast Asia and elsewhere' and deal with rogue states that support terrorism or trade in weapons of mass destruction. 'The most notorious rogue,' it said, 'is, without doubt, Saddam Hussein – proof if ever we needed it that yesterday's unfinished business becomes tomorrow's headache.' The article concluded:

> The events of September 11 are a terrible reminder that freedom demands eternal vigilance. And for too long we have not been vigilant. We have harboured those who hated us, tolerated those who threatened us and indulged those who weakened us. As a result, we remain, for example, all but defenceless against ballistic missiles that could be launched against our cities. A missile defence system will begin to change that. But change must go deeper still. The west as a whole needs to strengthen its resolve against rogue regimes and upgrade its defences. The good news is that America has a president who can offer the leadership necessary to do so.

'The West', according to an alternative view, needs to imagine an enemy for itself, a dangerous and malevolent being that must be fought and suppressed.[7] The supposed existence of a threatening enemy helps to maintain social cohesion and a certain deference towards political leaders, and helps to maintain public support for expenditure on substantial weapons programmes. It is proclaimed not only by political and military leaders but also in a myriad of popular films, TV programmes, novels, comics and computer games, and is a staple of everyday conversation wherever people meet, and on radio phone-in programmes and in internet chatrooms.

For several decades after 1945, the argument continues, the bogey figure in the West was the Soviet Union and, more generally, global communism. Earlier it had been other Western countries and, for several centuries, Europe had defined itself as essentially different from, and more civilised than, 'the Orient' and 'darkest Africa'. When the Iron Curtain came down, a new bogey had to be constructed. Folk memories of the Orient, the Crusades and the Ottoman Empire were brought out of storage, and were combined with resentment at the oil-based power of many Muslim countries.

It has been all the easier to sustain an image of Islam as deeply malevolent since so-called fundamentalists, extremists, militants, Islamists have played up to it and thereby confirmed people's worst fears with their acts of terrorism and lurid, westophobic denunciations of Western ways. The image has become additionally attractive, since it can be used to justify why Muslim communities in European countries should be prevented from moving out of the menial and low-status jobs for which they were originally recruited, and why Muslim demands for cultural and religious recognition within Europe should be resisted and rejected.

Combating Islamophobia within Britain necessarily involves engaging with the neo-conservative view of world affairs, sketched above, and with certain other alternative views. In Box 12 there are quotations from a range of writers about the current international situation. They do not share the neo-conservative view of international relations but they are ready to engage with it. Between them, they show the wider global context that has to be considered and discussed if Islamophobia in Britain is to be successfully combated.

The views and voices in Box 12 present a range of opinion. One of them calls explicitly, and the others call implicitly, for a 'great conversation' between and within cultures and civilisations. It will necessarily involve disagreements on many matters. The disagreements occur amongst Muslims talking with each other; and amongst non-Muslims talking with each other; and between Muslims and non-Muslims. How, in the great conversation, can criticisms and disagreements of Islam avoid feeding Islamophobia? This is the fundamental question considered in the next chapter.

Box 12

Great conversation
views and voices on international relations

Long overdue
We are long overdue for an open cultural exchange between Islam and the west in our own neighbourhoods. We desperately need a frank discussion with each other about who we are and what we believe – even if neither side likes what they hear...Even if bin Laden's network ceased to exist, we'd still have to confront the fact that two great civilisations, with a long history of conflict, are once again facing off in the global arena... Politicians, military commanders and journalists talk about the 'Great Game', a reference to the geopolitical intrigues being played out between Islam and the west in the Afghan war. What we need is 'The Great Conversation' between Islam and the west so we can figure out how to accommodate each other. Until we do, our world will continue to be a dangerous and precarious place.
Jeremy Rifkind, 'Dialogue is a necessity', The Guardian, 13 November 2001

Tough on terrorism and its causes
Our shock and outrage at the murder of the innocents in America on 11 September must not obscure a wider analysis and a wider sense of humanity. The murder and terror of civilians as policy does not begin with the acts of 11 September. If we attend to the news carefully, we will be reminded that they occur regularly in a number of places in the world, sometimes by, or at least supported by, western states. The perception of these victim populations is often that they matter less than when westerners are victims. It is this deep sense that the West is perceived by many to exercise double standards and that this is a source of grievance, hate and terrorism which is perhaps the most important lesson of 11 September, not the division of the world into rival civilisations, civilised and uncivilised, good and evil. This perception has to be addressed seriously if there is to be dialogue across countries, faiths and cultures, and foreign and security policies need to be reviewed in the light of the understanding that is achieved. Our security in the West, no less than that of any other part of the world, depends upon ... being tough on terrorism and tough on the causes of terrorism
Tariq Modood, in The Quest for Sanity, 2002

Must now become vocal
The magnitude of the terrorist attack on America has forced Muslims to take a critical look at themselves. Why have we repeatedly turned a blind eye to the evil within our societies? Why have we allowed the sacred terms of Islam, such as *fatwa* and *jihad*, to be hijacked by obscurantist, fanatic extremists?...If you see something reprehensible, said the Prophet Muhammad, then change it with your hand; if you are not capable of that then use your tongue (speak out against it); and if you are not capable of that then detest it in your heart. The silent Muslim majority must now become vocal. The rest of the world could help by adopting a more balanced tone.
Ziauddin Sardar, 'My fatwa on the fanatics', The Observer, 23 September 2001

There is a difference between knowledge of other peoples and other times that is the result of understanding, compassion, careful study and analysis for their own sakes, and on the other hand knowledge – if that is what is – that is part of an overall campaign of self-affirmation, belligerency and outright war. There is, after all, a profound difference between the will to understand for purposes of co-existence and humanistic enlargement of horizons, and the will to dominate for the purposes of control and external dominion.
Edward Said, preface to Orientalism, 2003 edition

A kind of cleansing
We'd better acknowledge the sheer danger of religiousness. Yes, it can be a tool to reinforce diseased perceptions of reality. Muslim or not, it can be a way of teaching ourselves not to see the particular human agony in front of us; or worse, of teaching ourselves not to see ourselves, our violence, our actual guilt as opposed to our abstract 'religious' sinfulness. Our religious talking, seeing, knowing, needs a kind of cleansing.
Rowan Williams, Writing in the Dust, 2002

The interests of anthropology
Anthropology has much for which to thank bin Laden... Anthropology was on the ropes. Like John Keats's knight in *La Belle Dame Sans Merci* it appeared to be 'ailing' and 'alone and palely loitering'. September 11 changed all that. The main interests of anthropology – ideas of ethnicity, group loyalty, honour, revenge, suicide, tribal code, the conflict between what anthropologists call the Great Tradition of world religions and their local practice or the Little Tradition – were being discussed everywhere.
Akbar Ahmed, Islam Under Siege, 2003

4. CLOSED AND OPEN
Approaches to disagreement

Summary

It is sometimes claimed that use of the word 'Islamophobia' is a way of stifling legitimate debate and disagreement. This chapter starts by quoting a colourful statement of this view and continues by discussing and clarifying the differences between 'closed' and 'open' views of Islam amongst non-Muslims. It points out also that the closed/open distinction is relevant to disagreements within communities as well as between them, and to Muslim views of 'the West' as well as non-Muslim views of Islam.

No longer argue?

'Can we no longer even argue with a Muslim?' asked a headline in October 2002 over an article by Peter Hitchens in the *Mail on Sunday*. The article was about someone who had been charged with 'religiously aggravated threatening behaviour' following an altercation with his Muslim neighbour. The columnist robustly criticised the police and political correctness – 'the constabulary is terrified of being accused of institutional racism and would probably charge a brick wall with harassment if a Muslim drove into it' – and also the new legislation under which the man was charged.[1]

Further, Hitchens had a go at the Crown Prosecution Service, the Human Rights Act and the prime minister's wife: 'This is a new crime invented in the mad, hysterical weeks after the Twin Towers outrage... During this period most politicians simply took leave of their senses, which is presumably why the enemies of free speech in the Home Office chose this opportunity to slip it past them. As for the CPS, this incident proves that it's not just dim and useless but nasty as well ... The CPS, which cannot defend the public against crime, is fully signed up to the anti-British, intolerant speech codes of Comrade Cherie Blair and her friends ...The authorities are far more effective at policing ideas than at suppressing crime. Perhaps the CPS should in future have a new name. How about Thought Police?'

The headline – 'Can we no longer argue with a Muslim?' – was rather lost sight of as the article continued. It was a useful way, however, of posing an extremely important set of issues. Is it really the case that criticising Islam is not acceptable and may even be unlawful? Does action against Islamophobia involve being uncritical towards Islam? The reply to both questions must, of course, be no. There is all the difference in the world between reasoned criticism and disagreement concerning certain aspects of Islam, and blind hatred against all of Islam. However (see Box 7), this distinction is frequently lost in polemical writings by journalists and commentators – even when they explicitly claim that they are not referring to all Muslims but only to some.

In 2002, for example, the author Martin Amis provoked uproar with his thoughts on Islam. Speaking at the Orange Word Festival on 20 October 2002, he said: 'It seems to me that the key to radical Islam is that it is quivering with male insecurity. It's an equation that never works out. There's a huge injection of sexuality – men's sexuality – in radical Islam.' There was an angry reaction from Muslim academics and religious leaders. Dr Ghada Karmi, vice-president of the Council for the Advancement of Arab-British Understanding, told *The Times* (21/10/02) that Amis had joined 'the steadily growing band of critics of Islam 'who disguised their position by pretending to only criticise radical Islam. This idea about sexuality is quite clearly a headline-grabber.' She added: 'It is fashionable to make outrageous comments about Islam and this is an outrageous comment. It is nonsense. I would have thought Martin Amis would not need any more publicity. This sort of comment is sensationalist and betrays considerable ignorance on the part of the people who make it.'

Even more offensive was an article by the iconoclastic art and social commentator Brian Sewell. His article 'Militant Islam is Placing a Noose Around the Globe', published in the *Evening Standard* (22/10/02), did not even attempt to differentiate between some Muslims and all Muslims. 'Whatever gentle scholars say of Islam as a pious submission to the will of God, however much they point to Arab mathematics, medicine and astronomy, poetry and architecture, metalwork and manuscript, the fact remains that Islam has always been militant; the urge to conquer and convert began with the great imperial thrust of Mohammed himself and was given impetus by his sudden death in 632AD.'

Sewell warned there could be worse to come: 'If Islam chooses in defence of its values to explode more bombs or crash more planes in the great cities of the West and its holiday resorts, it can bring us to a halt. It needs no extravagance of armies and their armaments, no mad Mahdis and their dervishes – just the touch of sudden slaughter in Southend and San Francisco, a Boeing crashed, a cruising liner holed, for by such means Islam can reduce the West to a hapless dog maddened by a swarm of wasps.'

Again, the reaction was swift. In a letter of complaint to the newspaper, Inayat Bunglawala of the Muslim Council of Britain noted that Sewell called on the west to 'understand the history, culture and values of Islam', but regretted that he 'seems to exclude himself from this noble aim.' But the damage had been done. Hundreds of thousands of people must have seen and been influenced by Sewell's high-profile article. Far fewer would have seen the letter of complaint and correction.

'Mindless Islamophilia'

In *The Guardian* (18/9/01) Julie Burchill drew an interesting and potentially valuable distinction between what she called 'mindless Islamophobia' and 'mindless Islamophilia'. She appeared, however, to think that the latter is considerably more prevalent and serious than the former and directed virtually all her polemic at fellow journalists who try to counter Islamophobia by presenting positive images of Islam in their work. She mocked the BBC for giving airspace to what she called a strong Muslim woman

(SMW for short), and for systematically implying that 'British Empire = bad' whereas 'Islamic Empire = good'. There was no mention during the BBC's recent Islam Week, she complained, of 'the women tortured, the Christian converts executed, the apostates hounded, the slaves in Sudan being sold into torment right now.' She continued: 'Call me a filthy racist – go on, you know you want to – but we have reason to be suspicious of Islam and treat it differently from the other major religions ... While the history of the other religions is one of moving forward out of oppressive darkness and into tolerance, Islam is doing it the other way round.'

Burchill's emotive generalisations and imagery ('oppressive darkness') were deeply offensive. Her claim that she was being rational, however, ('we have reason...') was interesting and worth attending to. For clearly there is such a thing as legitimate criticism and suspicion of religious beliefs and practices, even if Burchill's colourful language implied that she was not herself in this instance engaging in it. In castigating both mindless Islamophobia and mindless Islamophilia she was commending a stance that is mindful. Such a stance is suspicious when suspicion is warranted. But also it is ready, as appropriate, to respect and appreciate.

Closed and open views

In its 1997 report, the Commission on British Muslims and Islamophobia grappled with the problems that Burchill raised. When and how is it legitimate for non-Muslims to disagree with Muslims? How can you tell the difference between legitimate disagreement on the one hand and phobic dread and hatred on the other? In answer to such questions, the commission suggested that an essential distinction needs to be made between what it called *closed* views of Islam on the one hand and *open* views on the other. 'Phobic' hostility towards Islam is the recurring characteristic of closed views. Legitimate disagreement and criticism, as also appreciation and respect, are aspects of open views.

In summary form, the distinctions between closed and open views are to do with:

- whether Islam is seen as monolithic, static and authoritarian, or as diverse and dynamic with substantial internal debates

- whether Islam is seen as totally 'other', separate from the so-called West, or as both similar and interdependent, sharing a common humanity and a common space

- whether Islam is seen as inferior, backward and primitive compared with the so-called West, or as different but equal

- whether Islam is seen as an aggressive enemy to be feared, opposed and defeated, or as a cooperative partner with whom to work on shared problems, locally, nationally and internationally

- whether Muslims are seen as manipulative, devious and self-righteous in their religious beliefs, or as sincere and genuine

- whether Muslim criticisms of the so-called West are rejected out of hand or whether they are considered and debated

- whether double standards are applied in descriptions and criticisms of Islam and the so-called West, or whether criticisms are even-handed

- whether no account is taken of the fact that Muslims have far less access to the media than non-Muslims, and are therefore at a competitive disadvantage on an uneven playing-field, or whether unequal freedom of expression is recognised

- whether anti-Muslim comments, stereotypes and discourse are seen as natural and 'common sense', or as problematic and to be challenged.

The words 'open' and 'closed' were derived from the title of a classic work on the psychology of dogmatism, *The Open and Closed Mind* by Milton Rokeach, first published in 1960. Rokeach was interested not primarily in the content of bigoted people's minds but in how their minds worked. Open-minded people are ready to change their views both of others and of themselves in the light of new facts and evidence, and are fair-minded in the sense that they do not caricature or over-generalise, and do not claim greater certainty than is warranted. Open-mindedness and fair-mindedness are components of what is sometimes termed civility, or moderation, or the middle way. 'At the heart of the concept of the middle

way,' writes a member of the Association of Muslim Social Scientists, 'is the principle of fairness, the "fair play" so integral to the English conception of good character.' He continues:

> Let us be clear about the origin of the English word 'fair', because it shows ... how closely this idea is connected to Islamic principles. The English word 'fair' has two meanings: the first is 'just, equitable, reasonable', and the second is 'beautiful'. But the meaning of the original Germanic root is 'fitting', that which is the right size, in the correct ratio or proportion. The range of meanings of this word 'fair' reflects a truly Islamic concept, the idea that to be just is to 'do what is beautiful' (*ihsan*), to act in accordance with our original nature (*fitra*), which God has shaped in just proportions (Qur'an 82:7) as a fitting reflection of divine order and harmony.

'The core issue,' writes someone on the basis of observing issues of religious affiliation in Scotland, 'is whether minds are closed – viewing other religions (or all religions) as being alien harmful monoliths, or whether they are open – to the facts of diversity, in which religious communities are given respect as people who are sincere in belief, morality and desire to become full partners in political and civic enterprise.'[2] She goes on to stress that it is not only individuals who have closed or open minds but also groups and communities: 'Within every world religious community, whether Christian, Jewish or Muslim, the open and the closed views are in contention. The open communities seek alliance and partnership; extremists of the closed tendency form cliques, factions and sects that can resort to militant action. The 'closed' extremists terrorise their co-religionists along with all the others who stand in their way.'

The distinction between open and closed minds corresponds to the distinction which Akbar Ahmed, writing as a professional anthropologist, draws between inclusivism and exclusivism. (There is a brief quotation from Ahmed's *Islam Under Siege* in Box 12). In the first instance Ahmed is referring to two different ways in which Muslims themselves understand and practise their religion, and relate to others. But his distinctions also apply to 'the West'. He writes:

Exclusivists create boundaries and believe in hierarchies; inclusivists are those who are prepared to accommodate, to interact with others, and even listen to them and be influenced by them.

Inclusivists are those who believe that human civilisation is essentially one, however much we are separated by religion, culture or language.

...I believe the real battle in the 21st century will be between the inclusivists and the exclusivists.[3]

Self-criticism and recognising diversity

Professor Ahmed's remarks stress that the closed and open distinction applies to everyone – Muslims in their views of 'the West' as also non-Muslims in their views of Islam. Further, he stresses that openness is a quality which a person has towards their own traditions and community as well as towards others. It therefore sometimes involves self-criticism. Also, it necessarily involves a readiness to engage with 'the Other', and to co-operate with others in building a common life.[4]

'Saddam Hussein was, and remains, a product of our own culture,' writes a British Muslim. 'While much more brutal, he is not that much different from all the other despots in the Arab world. We need to ask why Muslim societies are so prone to despotism and dictatorships, still so deeply anchored in feudalism and tribalism. Are we getting the leaders we deserve? Why is routine torture so prevalent in Muslim societies? Why are basic human rights, including the rights of women, so starkly missing from Islamic societies? What role have we played and are we playing in our own destruction? These are uncomfortable questions. We do everything to try and avoid them...We would much rather wallow in nostalgia, recount the glories of our 'Golden Age', and insist on how Islam provides an answer to everything, than take an objective and critical look at our own shortcomings.'[5]

Such self-criticism necessarily goes hand in hand with recognising diversity within one's own culture. The author whose self-criticism is quoted above is also the author who writes eloquently about diversity within Islam in the extract in Box 13.[6]

Box 13

The art of generosity
Islam as a garden

I think we Muslims need to rediscover the art of generosity. We need to realise that Islam is much bigger than our own, inevitably blinkered, outlook and amenable to multiple interpretations. We need to stop thinking about Islam as though it was some sort of desert where only one arid interpretation dominates.

Instead, we should think of Islam as a garden. Gardens, by the very fact that they are gardens, consist of a plethora of different plants. There are varieties of hardy perennials that flower year after year. Annuals and biennials that have to be planted in season. Plants that provide colours of foliage, or hedges and borders, or climb up fences, or play architectural roles. There are fruit trees, trees that provide fragrant and colourful flowers, and trees that fix the soil and provide shade. There are the grasses so essential for the lawns. And what would a garden be without the proverbial birds and bees? And those worms and insects that both enrich the soil and require some form of pest control.

The thing about a garden is that all this truly monumental variety of life exits in symbiosis: nourishing each other and ensuring the overall survival of the garden. Of course the garden has to be tended: the weeds have to be cleared, plants have to be pruned, we have to make sure that nothing over-grows – that is, no single interpretation becomes an overarching, totalitarian ideology so much that it ends up suffocating and endangering other plants. Not for nothing is the garden the central metaphor of the Islamic paradise!

So, rejoice in manifold interpretations of Islam and in your multiple Selfs. Be impossible. Be traditionalist or modern, Deobandi or Baralavi, Sufi or Salafi – but above all, be generous. Let others flourish as much as you would like to flourish yourself. Let the numerous interpretations of Islam, the vast variety of Muslim cultures, past, present and future, exist in symbiosis as though Islam was a global garden.

As for me, I get a sadistic pleasure out of terrifying people. And I do not have to do anything to achieve it. I just have to be myself.

Source: 'Cultivating the Soil' by Ziauddin Sardar, Emel Magazine, September 2003

'A culture cannot appreciate the values of others,' remarks Bhikhu Parekh, 'unless it appreciates the plurality within it ... A culture cannot be at ease with its differences from others unless it is also at ease with its own internal differences.'[7]

As she stood down in 2002 as UN High Commissioner for Human Rights, Mary Robinson said that for all the warnings, the phenomenon of Islamophobia has spread throughout the United States and Western Europe. 'When we speak of Islam', said Robinson, 'we are speaking of the religion of over 20 per cent of the human population spread across the globe and expressed through many cultures. It is important to recognise the greatness of Islam, its

civilisations and its immense contributions to the richness of the human experience.' This stress on diversity is a hallmark of what above is called an 'open' view of Islam. The same stress is seen in the views expressed in Box 14. These too recognise the diversity of Islam. At the same time they readily acknowledge diversity within 'the West' and do so with self-criticism. They make an impressive reply to the negativity in Box 6. And interestingly, one of them contributed to the kinds of comment quoted in Box 6 and is writing now to express shame and regret.

Box 14

Solidarity at this time
Messages to the Muslim Council of Britain, September 2001 – April 2003

I heard on the news today that you had been receiving hate mail since the terrible news about America broke on 11th September. I'm not surprised that extreme racists would take advantage of such an awful situation to peddle their hate. But I am saddened that some of the general public and indeed the media don't seem to be able to differentiate between those who committed these crimes, who may or may not be Muslim, and anyone who just happens to be Muslim. That is worrying. I would like to express my solidarity with you at this sad and unpleasant time. (12/9/01)

I have just been reading some of the emails sent to you by people of this country. It makes me ashamed. It is not as though 'white' English people have not committed any crimes as evil as this. All communities have their evil people, you are not alone there. (14/9/01)

Just after the attack on 9/11 I am ashamed to say I sent you one of those hate-emails you had so many of. It was unfair of me, and I should not have done it. What upset me, what made me so angry, were the pictures of those Palestinians celebrating the deaths of so many innocent people. I couldn't reach them so I took my hurt out on you. Please accept my sincere apologies. (10/10/01)

I would like to thank all those people who have reached out to the Muslim community in this difficult hour. I feel immense joy in hearing the encouragement and empathy resounding from so many corners of this country. It is great to realise that there are a lot of good people out there who selflessly stand up for the greater good. God bless you all! (9/10/01)

I am worried that the UK media continues to churn out news reports and programmes that whip up misunderstanding against the Muslim community worldwide and in the UK. The dangerous equation is being made that Islam = terrorism. It reminds me of the blind propaganda that that Nazis pumped out against the Jews in Europe. We had our people attacked in the street, our women abused, bearded Jews attacked by Nazi mobs and forced to shave, and finally we were sent to the death camps. I will not stand by and tolerate any of my Muslim brothers being abused. (15/10/01)

I write to show solidarity with my Moslem brothers and sisters. I am an Irish Catholic and it is totally contrary to all Christian principles for such a war as this to be waged against humanity. I am joining in prayer vigils and peace marches to let my voice be heard along with millions of others around the world. (25/3/03)

Source: www.mcb.org.uk

Concluding note

The themes of this chapter are taken up later in the book. The distinction between open and closed views is fundamental in all considerations of media coverage (chapter 10) and is essential in teaching about Islam and 'the West' in schools (chapter 8). Also, it is crucial in community cohesion programmes (chapter 9).

Inclusivism, open-mindedness and the middle way cannot be compelled by law. The law can, however, encourage and foster them. Alternatively, alas, the law can be unhelpful and unsupportive. The potential of UK law, with particular regard to recognising British Muslim identities, is discussed in chapters 6 and 7.

First, in the next chapter, the importance of recognising Muslim identity in the census of population is considered, and there is information about the findings in 2001 about the socio-economic position of British Muslims.

5. COUNTING
Recognition and religion

Summary

This chapter begins with a discussion of the political and legal concept of recognition. It then recalls that there was a question about religious affiliation in the 2001 census and cites some of the findings that have so far been published, focusing in particular on disadvantage and social exclusion.

It may cause you injury

> Ladies and gentlemen, we are about to land at Heathrow. Please stow away your tray tables, put your seats in the upright position, ensure your seatbelt is securely fastened and that your racial identity is put away carefully in a safe place as otherwise it may well pop out and cause you injury.

Thus the Black British writer Gary Younge imagines an announcement on the plane's tannoy system as he returns to Britain from the United States.[1] He tells it how it is for most Black British people. Change 'racial identity' to 'religious identity' or cultural identity' and he's telling how it is for British Muslims. And change it to 'gender', 'sexual identity' or 'national identity', and he's speaking for many others. There are millions of people in Britain who would dearly like their identity to be recognised and respected in public, instead of being invisible, derided or despised. But being invisible, when push comes to shove, is preferable to be being actually attacked.

Disposition of the eyes

When they approach me they see only my surroundings, themselves, or figments of their imagination – indeed everything and anything except me ... That invisibility to which I refer occurs because of a peculiar disposition of the eyes of those with whom I come in contact. A matter of the construction of their inner eyes, those eyes with which they look through their physical eyes upon reality.

Ralph Ellison, *The Invisible Man.*

'The politics of recognition', as it is sometimes known, is of increasing importance in modern democracies[2]. An alternative phrase is 'the politics of difference'. People want and expect to be treated equally, most certainly. That's what democracy is all about. But also they want profound and precious aspects of their identity to be seen, heard and respected, and in that sense they want to be treated differently. 'Due recognition,' writes the Canadian philosopher Charles Taylor, 'is not just a courtesy we owe people. It is a vital human need.' Islamophobia in modern Britain, as also in other Western democracies, prevents that vital need from being fulfilled. But to meet and fulfil the need, by the same token, is a vital way of combating and reducing Islamophobia.

Nonrecognition and misrecognition

Identity is partly shaped by recognition or its absence, often by the misrecognition of others, and so a person or group of people or society can suffer real damage, real distortion, if the people or society around them mirror back to them a confining or demeaning or contemptible picture of themselves. Nonrecognition or misrecognition can inflict harm, can be a form of oppression, imprisoning someone in a false, distorted and reduced mode of being.

Charles Taylor, *The Politics of Recognition*

Recognition in the census

One obvious place where recognition is essential is the national census of population. It was largely due to tireless and skilful lobbying by many Muslim organisations through the 1990s, robustly supported by the Inter Faith Network and a range of Christian organisations, that the 2001 census contained a

Table 1: Religious affiliations in the United Kingdom

Religion	England	Scotland	Wales	Northern Ireland	UK Total	UK %
Buddhist	139,046	6,830	5,407	533	151,816	0.3
Christian	35,251,244	3,294,545	2,087,242	1,446,386	42,079,417	71.6
Hindu	546,982	5,564	5,439	825	558,810	1.0
Jewish	257,671	6,448	2,256	365	266,740	0.5
Muslim	1,524,887	42,557	21,739	1,943	1,591,126	2.7
Sikh	327,343	6,572	2,015	219	336,149	0.6
Other religions	143,811	26,974	6,909	1,143	178,837	0.3
Total all religions	38,190,984	3,389,490	2,131,007	1,451,414	45,162,895	76.8
No religion	7,171,332	1,394,460	537,935		9,103,727	15.5
Not stated	3,776,515	278,061	234,143		4,288,719	7.3
All no religion or not stated	10,947,847	1,672,521	772,078	233,853	13,392,436	23.2

Source: Office for National Statistics, London; General Register Office, Scotland; Northern Ireland Statistics and Research Agency. Collated by the Inter Faith Network, 2003.

question about religious affiliation[3]. Government officials argued that religion belongs in the personal sphere, but faith communities contended that their religion often has a significant impact on their interaction with society as a whole, for example in the quality of public services they receive. After years of wrangling, it was agreed that the question 'What is your religion?' should be a voluntary one – the only voluntary question on the census form. It was answered by 92.7 per cent of respondents.

The campaign to include the question began in the build up to the 1991 Census, but intensified four years later. It eventually gained support from various government departments. In December 1998, at a reception given by the Muslim Council of Britain, the Home Secretary (then Jack Straw) made a crucially important announcement: 'I think it is becoming clear that more people are identifying themselves in terms of their religion or culture than ever before. That is why there is a need to expand on the kind of ethnic monitoring that is carried out in the Census. The basic classifications of black, white or Asian are simply out of date.'

In making this statement, the Home Secretary was in effect accepting and underlining fundamental distinctions that were made during the campaign between 'beliefs', 'practice' and 'affiliation'. The census question was not about people's personal religious beliefs, nor about whether they observed a religion by, for example, attending worship or

following certain practices. Rather, it was about their affiliation, the community they identified with. Recognising in the census the importance for many citizens of religious affiliation was a significant step forward in Britain's understanding of itself.

Following the government's explicit commitment and further intensive behind-the-scenes lobbying, the Census Amendment Bill was presented to the House of Commons in June 2000 and passed by 194 votes to 10. The following year the censuses for England and Wales, Scotland and Northern Ireland all included slightly differing voluntary questions on religion. Six world faiths were mentioned on the form in England and Wales and in addition people could write in any other religion if they wished and could also indicate that they had no religion. As mentioned above, the question was voluntary and about four million people chose not to answer it. Table 1 shows the distribution of answers across the UK's four nations.

Overall, almost a quarter of the population said on their census forms that they had no religion, or else did not answer the question. The vast majority (94 per cent) who did not state their religion were white, as were almost four fifths (78 per cent) of those who ticked the 'any other religion' box. Of the 76 per cent of people who did answer with a religious category, 72 identified themselves as Christian. With regard to people whose affiliation was to a religion other than Christianity, there is fuller information in Table 2. It shows that of those who did not describe themselves

Table 2: Religions in England and Wales other than Christianity

Religion	Total	% of non-Christian
Muslim	1,546.626	51.8
Hindu	552,421	18.5
Sikh	329,358	11.0
Jewish	259,927	8.7
Buddhist	144,453	4.8
Other	150,720	5.0

as Christian, just over a half identified themselves as Muslims. Almost a fifth were Hindus and just over a tenth Sikh. The Muslim community was shown to be larger than all other non-Christian communities put together.

Religion and ethnicity

Nearly all Hindus and Sikhs had an Indian heritage, and nearly all Jewish people described themselves as white. In the case of Muslims and Buddhists, however, there was much greater variation in the connection between religion and ethnicity, as shown in Table 3. For example, 35 per cent of Buddhists are white, 24 per cent are Chinese and 24 per cent ticked the 'other ethnic group' box on the census form. The Muslim community in Britain is substantially larger but is similarly diverse. Just over two thirds of British Muslims are of South Asian heritage – 42 per cent Pakistani, 17 per cent Bangladeshi and 8 per cent Indian. Almost 12 per cent are white (5 per cent of

UK heritage, 7 per cent other white heritages), and eight per cent are black (mostly of African heritage).

Nationally, as shown in Table 3, just over two thirds of British Muslims have their origins in Bangladesh, India or Pakistan. In London, however, the proportion is almost exactly a half. Thirty per cent of all Muslims in London belong to what the Office of National Statistics calls 'other' so far as ethnicity is concerned. It is also relevant to note that most British Muslims who belong to the 'white' categories (4.1 per cent 'white UK' and 7.5 per cent 'white other') live in London.

In the overall context of this report, the column in Table 3 about British Muslims is extremely significant, for it strikingly shows that Islam in Britain, as indeed Islam world-wide, is a multi-ethnic community. This point has far-reaching implications for the legal system and anti-discrimination legislation, as stressed and discussed in chapters 6 and 7.

Location

Table 4 lists the 14 authorities with the highest proportions of Muslims.

There are 24 cities or authorities in the UK which have at least 10,000 Muslim residents. About 75 per cent of all British Muslims live in these 24 places. Two fifths of all British Muslims live in London. The boroughs with the highest numbers are (in order) Tower Hamlets, Newham, Brent, Waltham Forest, Redbridge, Hackney, Haringey, Camden and

Table 3: Religion and ethnicity in England and Wales

	% of Buddhists	% of Christians	% of Hindus	% of Jews	% of Muslims	% of Sikhs
White (UK)	34.9	92.6	1.0	84.0	4.1	1.9
White other	3.1	2.3	0.2	12.4	7.5	0.2
Mixed	3.2	0.9	1.0	1.2	4.1	0.8
Bangladeshi	0.1	0.1	0.3	0.0	16.8	0.0
Indian	1.3	0.1	84.5	0.3	8.5	91.5
Pakistani	0.1	0.0	0.1	0.1	42.5	0.1
Other Asian	8.1	0.1	11.7	0.3	5.8	4.6
Caribbean	0.7	1.1	0.3	0.2	0.3	0.0
African	0.2	1.0	0.2	0.1	6.2	0.1
Chinese	23.7	0.1	0.0	0.0	0.0	0.0
Other	23.6	0.2	0.5	1.0	3.6	0.7
Totals	100	100	100	100	100	100
Base	144,453	37,338,486	552,421	259,927	1,546,626	329,358

Source: Census, April 2001, Office for National Statistics. Please note that not all ethnic categories are included.

TABLE 4: Local authorities in England with the highest proportion of Muslims

Local authority	Number of Muslim residents	Proportion of residents who are Muslim
Tower Hamlets	71,383	36.4
Newham	47,673	24.3
Blackburn	26,670	19.4
Waltham Forest	32,904	15.1
Luton	26,955	14.6
Birmingham	140,017	14.3
Hackney	27,909	13.8
Pendle	11,986	13.4
Slough	15,895	13.6
Brent	32,301	12.3
Redbridge	28,493	11.9
Westminster	21,337	11.8
Camden	22,911	11.6
Haringey	24,379	11.3

Westminster. (See Table 4). The proportions within each of these boroughs range from 36 per cent in the case of Tower Hamlets to 11 per cent in Haringey.

The region with the next highest proportion of all Muslims in the UK (14 per cent of all Muslims) is the West Midlands. There are four authorities here with more than 10,000 Muslim residents: Birmingham, Walsall, Sandwell and Coventry. There are almost as many (13 per cent) in the north west, where the authorities with at least 10,000 residents are Manchester, Blackburn, Oldham, Rochdale, Bolton, Pendle and Preston. The Yorkshire and Humber region has 12 per cent of all Muslims in the UK. The authorities here with the largest numbers are Bradford, Kirklees, Sheffield, Leeds and Calderdale.

Age

Age profiles differ greatly between Muslim communities and the population as a whole. Just over a third of all Muslims (33.8 per cent) are aged 0-15, and almost a fifth (18.2 per cent) are aged 16-24. The national average is 20.2 per cent aged 0-15 and 10.9 per cent aged 16-24. Since Muslim communities have proportionately more young people than the national average they are bound to grow in size, both proportionately and absolutely, over the next 20 years.

Poverty and social exclusion

Many children in Britain live in 'workless' households with over two million (17.6 per cent) in households where there are no adults in work. In Muslim households the proportion is even higher, with more than a third of children living in households where no adults have work. Muslim children also experience much more overcrowding: more than two in five – 41.7 per cent compared with an average of 12.3 per cent – and one in eight live in a household with no central heating compared with the average of 5.9 per cent, one in sixteen. Three quarters of Bangladeshi and Pakistani children live in household earning less than half the national average. Poverty is such that 54 per cent of their homes survive on income support.

The rates of poor health among Pakistani, Bangladeshi and 'other Asian' people are all well above average when analysed by age group. Among men aged 50-64 and with a limiting long-term illness the average proportion overall reporting their health as 'not good' is 13.7per cent. Among Bangladeshi men this figure is 30.9 per cent and among Pakistani men 26.3 per cent.

Pakistani and Bangladeshi communities have much lower employment rates and higher unemployment rates than national averages – 31 per cent of Pakistani men aged 16-74 are full-time employees, 14.2 per cent are self-employed, and 9.1 per cent are unemployed. The corresponding figures for Bangladeshi men are 23.1 per cent full-time employees, 9 per cent self-employed, and 10.2 per cent unemployed. When Muslim men do find employment, the playing field remains skewed against them. Average earnings among Muslim men are 68 per cent of that taken home by non-Muslims.

A high proportion of Pakistani and Bangladeshi women aged 16-74 look after the home and family – 36.4 per cent of Pakistani women and 40.1 per cent of Bangladeshi women, compared to the average of 11.9 per cent for England and Wales[4].

6. CRIMINAL JUSTICE

Hate crime, policing, courts, prisons

Summary

This chapter looks first at how Muslims are treated when they are the victims or targets of hate crime – violence, harassment, incitement and abuse. Second, it looks at the experience of Muslims when they are alleged or convicted offenders. It notes that there have been significant improvements in recent years in how Muslims are treated when they are victims or targets. These are to an extent offset, however, by widespread perceptions in British Muslim communities that there is unfair treatment in policing, sentencing and prisons.

Racist and religious violence

As the 1997 report on Islamophobia was being written, the government was preparing its crime and disorder bill. This included legislation whereby greater penalties would be applied in four areas of crime if the offence were shown by the prosecution to be aggravated by racism. The four areas were assaults and violence; damage to property; harassment; and threatening, abusive and insulting behaviour. The report recommended that the legislation should also make reference to religious as well as racist aggravation. The recommendation was rejected at the time but was subsequently accepted. Later, the concept of religious aggravation was applied across all categories of crime.

In 2002 the European Centre on Racism and Xenophobia warned, from widespread anecdotal evidence, of a rise in Islamophobic violence.[1] The Islamic Human Rights Commission logged 674 cases in the year following September 2001, including instances of abuse, discrimination, harassment and violence. Many cases involved Muslim women having their scarves forcibly pulled off or having alcohol thrown at them. In one incident a schoolgirl had her headscarf pulled off by a parent of another child at the school gates – to the sound of laughter by those watching. There were clubbing incidents with bats, an attack on a child with pepper spray and a Muslim was deliberately run over by a car. The IHRC noted that women and children had been particularly targeted and many victims had little confidence in the police.

This in itself, it pointed out, would consequently put them, the victims, in a more vulnerable position.

Ahmed Versi, editor of *The Muslim News,* observed that while the war with Iraq triggered fewer cases of abuse than 9/11, concern remains high: 'We have reported cases of mosques being firebombed, paint being thrown at mosques, mosques being covered with graffiti, threats made, women being spat upon, eggs being thrown. It is the visible symbols of Islam that are being attacked. History is being repeated. People should learn from history but there is no recognition of what is happening.'[2]

The phrase in Scottish law: 'aggravated by religious prejudice' is clearer than the equivalent phrase in English law: 'religiously aggravated'. In Scotland the measure was introduced only after thorough consultation and deliberation. It was accordingly well thought through and there was substantial public understanding and support. In England, however, the legal change was made as a result of a brief reference in the Anti-Terrorism, Crime and Security Act. It was widely seen as a sop to Muslim opinion, to compensate for measures whose effect would be to curtail the civil liberties of certain Muslims, rather than because the government was genuinely committed to recognising Muslim identity.

As of September 2003 the Crown Prosecution Service (CPS) had received only 40 'religiously aggravated' cases from the police. The offences ranged from common assault to a case of attempted murder. Most cases involved minor assaults, public order offences or criminal damage. There had been eleven convictions. These small numbers compare with 4,201 cases of racially aggravated crime received in the year ending March 2003, and 3,123 prosecutions.

The CPS published a formal policy statement on racist and religious crime on 14 July 2003 with the aim of raising awareness of the issues throughout the criminal justice system. The result is likely to be that more offences will be reported and prosecuted. Attorney General Lord Goldsmith QC, speaking at the launch of the policy, stressed that 'a racially or religiously motivated attack is an attack on the whole community. This policy sends a clear message to perpetrators that they will not get away with threatening, violent or abusive behaviour.'

Threats, offence and incitement to hatred

The concept of incitement to racial hatred has its origins in deliberations and concerns leading to the Public Order Act 1936. The Act was a measure to combat the marches and mass meetings organised in the 1930s by the British Union of Fascists (BUF), led by Sir Oswald Mosley. It had two principal intentions, corresponding to two separate harms that it wished to prevent:

- to ban activities that were likely – or, indeed, intended – to encourage or provoke people taking part in them to commit hate crimes against the members of certain communities, particularly the Jewish community

- to reduce distress, intimidation and anger in the communities, mainly Jewish, against which the BUF organised, spoke and marched.

The two sets of harms were clearly connected with each other. In the heat and hurly-burly of a street battle they were all but indistinguishable. Nevertheless they are different from each other from a legal point of view and only the first can properly be described as being to do with incitement, as distinct from causing offence and intimidation. In 1965, when incitement to racial hatred came explicitly on to the statute book, the second purpose in the original legislation was unfortunately de-emphasised. Similarly it was de-emphasised in the Race Relations Act 1976. However, it was indirectly alluded to by a requirement in the

Public Order Act and the Race Relations Act that incitement had to be 'threatening, abusive or insulting' for a prosecution to be brought.

But these three key words were not defined. Nor was the assumed connection explained between (a) inciting and (b) being abusive. (A person can be highly abusive and threatening without intending or being likely to incite hate crimes. By the same token, there can be incitement to hate crimes without any use of threats or insults.) It is primarily because of the lack of clarity in the law and confusion between the two different sets of harms, but also because of uncertainty about how it co-exists with the right to freedom of expression, that prosecutions for incitement to racial hatred over the years have been extremely rare.

The Crime and Disorder Act 1998 introduced the concept of 'racially aggravated', as mentioned above. It involved, amongst other things, an amendment to the section of the Public Order Act that deals with threatening, abusive or insulting behaviour. The second intention in the original 1936 legislation (see above) was now explicit. In autumn 2001, as a consequence of the Anti-Terrorism, Crime and Security Act, the phrase 'racially aggravated' was expanded to 'racially or religiously aggravated'. The great significance of this was not immediately appreciated for the principal debates and headlines were around the less important question of whether or not to amend the section of the Public Order Act dealing with incitement. (Less important, because the law on incitement was already ambiguous, as outlined above, and had seldom actually been used.)

The significance began to be apparent in summer 2003 with a landmark ruling at the High Court. The court handed down a judgement which involved drawing a distinction between (a) insulting the tenets of a religion and (b) insulting and intimidating its followers. The latter – 'threatening, abusing or insulting, within the hearing or sight of a person likely to be caused harassment, alarm or distress thereby' – may now be considered a religiously aggravated offence under the Public Order Act 1986, as amended by the Anti-Terrorism, Crime and Security Act 2001. Moreover, the High Court made clear that the amended legislation is not concerned narrowly with insulting people with a religious affiliation. Much more widely, if 'any right thinking member of society'

Box 15

Any right thinking member of society
– a landmark ruling

In November 2001 a member of the British National Party, Mark Norwood, put a small poster, 24 inches by 15 inches, on a first-floor front window of his flat in a rural town in Shropshire. The poster had been created by the BNP nationally and contained in large print the words 'Islam out of Britain' and 'Protect the British people'. It bore also a picture of one of the twin towers of the World Trade Centre in flames on 11 September, and a Crescent and Star surrounded by a prohibition sign. Norwood was fined £300 by Oswestry magistrates court under the Public Order Act 1986, section 5, for causing alarm or distress. The court deemed further that the offence was religiously aggravated.

The law states that 'a person is guilty of an offence if he ... displays any writing, sign or other visible representation which is threatening, abusive or insulting, within the hearing or sight of a person likely to be caused harassment, alarm or distress. An offence under this section may be committed in a public or a private place.'

Section 6 of the Act explains that 'a person is guilty of an offence under section 5 only if he intends ... the writing, sign or other visible representation to be threatening, abusive or insulting, or is aware that it may be threatening, abusive or insulting.'

The Act was amended in 1998 to include the concept of 'racially aggravated' and in 2000 this phrase was expanded into 'racially or religiously aggravated'. The law now states that an offence is racially or religiously aggravated if it is 'motivated (wholly or partly) by hostility towards members of a racial or religious group based on their membership of that group'.

Norwood appealed against his conviction. In a landmark ruling in July 2003, two High Court judges upheld the conviction. They rejected Norwood's arguments, supported by Nicolas Griffin, the chairman of the British National Party, that (a) the poster was not abusive or insulting; (b) there was no evidence of anyone having been harassed, alarmed or distressed; and (c) it was in any case a reasonable and legitimate exercise of freedom of speech under human rights legislation, namely Article 10.1 of the European Convention on Human Rights.

The Court ruled that the poster could not on any reasonable basis be dismissed as merely an intemperate criticism or protest against the tenets of the Muslim religion, as distinct from an unpleasant and insulting attack on its followers generally; and that the issue was whether distress was *likely* to be caused, not whether it had in fact been caused. Further, it re-emphasised that freedom of expression is not absolute but may be restricted for the prevention of disorder or crime and for the protection of the rights of others.

Norwood's defence quoted a judgment from a case in 1999 in which the judge had observed that free speech includes 'not only the inoffensive, but the irritating, the contentious, the eccentric, the heretical, the unwelcome and the provocative, provided that it does not tend to provoke violence. Freedom only to speak inoffensively is not worth having.' The case for the prosecution, in response to this, was that people may by all means criticise certain religious tenets or practices, but that Norwood was not entitled to display a poster whose real message was that 'the Islamic religion *and* its followers [italics in the original] are not welcome in the United Kingdom; that they should be kept out and/or removed; and that they pose a threat to the British people'. The High Court agreed. The poster, it said, 'was a public expression of attack on all Muslims in this country, urging all who might read it that followers of the Islamic religion here should be removed from it and warning that their presence here was a threat or a danger to the British people.'

This message, the prosecution argued, was likely to 'cause harassment, alarm or distress to any right-thinking member of society concerned with the preservation of peace and tolerance, and for the avoidance of religious and racial tension'. Such people include, but are not restricted to, followers of the Islamic religion. The High Court concurred with this argument.

Source: Judgement handed down by Lord Justice Auld and Mr Justice Goldring, Royal Courts of Justice, 3 July 2003

is likely to be caused harassment, alarm or distress by an attack on members of a specific religion, a public order offence has *prima facie* been committed. There is fuller information about this extremely important ruling in Box 15.

It is too early yet to foresee what the judgement referred to in Box 15 will lead to. No doubt there will be substantial debates aiming to clarify the meaning of 'any right thinking member of society', and around concepts of freedom of expression. 'Freedom to speak only inoffensively is not worth having,' it was said during the case described in Box 15, and presumably all right thinking members of society are expected to agree with this. The debates will be intricate and passionate. In the meanwhile, it is important to note that British Muslims do now have a substantial measure of protection from intemperate insults and abuse, as do the members of all other religions.

The High Court ruling may have little impact on thugs on the streets who have recently been replacing the word 'Paki' with the word 'Muslim' to explain to themselves who they think their targets are. But it will almost certainly restrain the tone of, for example, British National Party campaigning. There were no legal proceedings in summer 2002 when the BNP distributed leaflets containing sentiments that (a) were *prima facie* intended to stir up hostility towards Muslims and (b) were found by most or all Muslims, and most or all right thinking members of society, to be insulting, abusive and threatening. In future, however, in the light of the High Court ruling of July 2003, proceedings against such leaflets will no doubt be considered. The following extracts show the tone that the leaflets adopted.[3]

> 'It won't be long before Christianity is dead and buried and Britain becomes an Islamic dictatorship. After all, what can stop them? With continued immigration, high birthrates and conversions to Islam, Christianity is being crucified on the dark cross of multiculturalism and globalisation... Unless we change things Christianity in Britain is going to die.'

> 'Among the native British majority, no one dares to tell the truth about Islam and the way it threatens our democracy, traditional freedoms and identity – except for the British National Party. So

angry are the old parties about our willingness to stand up and tell the truth that they are about to rush new repressive 'laws' through Parliament to make exposing the evils of Islam an imprisonable offence.'

> 'Crazy, isn't it? Muslim rioters tear the town apart, attacking white people, houses and shops, and petrol-bombing and shooting at the police – and yet whites like us are getting the blame!'

> 'We've got to take action to put pressure on the Asian community to control the extremists and race-haters in their midst. Not by confrontation, but by boycotting their shops and take-aways. Not ones owned by Chinese or Hindus, only Muslims as it's their community we need to pressure.'

The amendment proposed in autumn 2001 to the section of the Public Order Act dealing with incitement (namely, the addition of the words 'and religious' to a law that was already poorly drafted and seldom used) would have been barely more than cosmetic. What is needed is a fundamental re-examination of the concept of incitement to hatred and to hate crimes, and of how it relates to causing offence and to freedom of expression. Until this time the judgement summarised in Box 15 is of great significance.

Freedom of expression and the nature of religion

In autumn 2001, when the proposal to make incitement to religious hatred unlawful was rejected, several speakers in the House of Lords took a view of religion that was at variance with the assumptions underlying the inclusion of a religious question in the census. (See the discussion in chapter 5.) They focused on beliefs and practice, and not on affiliation, and were thus able to argue that race and religion are substantially different concepts.

Race and religion are substantially different concepts, they argued, because a person cannot choose their race. They can, however, choose their religion and should be allowed to do so, and should be allowed to disavow religion entirely if that is their decision. The scientist Richard Dawkins expressed a view of religion that is widespread amongst intellectuals:

This is a Catholic baby. That is a Protestant baby. This is a Hindu baby. That is a Muslim baby. This baby thinks there are many gods. That baby is adamant that there is only one. But it is preposterous that we do this to children. They are too young to know what they think. To slap a label on a child at birth – to announce, in advance, as a matter of hereditary presumption if not determinate certainty, an infant's opinions on the cosmos and creation, on life and afterlives, on sexual ethics, abortion and euthanasia – is a form of mental child abuse.[4]

Similar arguments have been forcefully propounded by several commentators in the media. A flavour of them is given in Box 16.

The view that religious identity should be a matter of personal choice, not determined or given by factors beyond someone's personal control, is admittedly plausible and attractive at first sight. It makes ready sense to most agnostics and humanists such as Dawkins and the journalists quoted in Box 16, for their experience is that they freely choose not to hold religious beliefs or to engage in religious practices. It also makes sense to many religious people, for they too have freely chosen to embrace their beliefs.

If one considers religion as to do with affiliation rather than actual belief or practice, however, it is clear that the humanist polemics quoted above are misleading. For from this perspective religious identity is frequently not chosen and not primarily a matter of inner commitment to certain distinctively religious beliefs. On the contrary, many human beings are born into communities or identity groupings where various religious symbols are significant for maintaining a

---

Box 16

The only good religion
– religious hatred and freedom of expression

The only good religion

The only good religion is a moribund religion: only when the faithful are weak are they tolerant and peaceful. The horrible history of Christianity shows that whenever religion grabs temporal power it turns lethal. Those who believe theirs is the only way, truth and light will kill to create their heavens on earth if they get the chance. Tolerance only thrives when religion is banished to the private sphere, but bizarrely this government is marching backwards, with more faith schools, more use of 'faith communities' and now Blunkett's new laws against 'religious hatred' to save religion from vulgar abuse.

... The present danger is caused by Islamist theocracy. There is no point in pretending it is not so. Wherever Islam either is the government or bears down upon the government, it imposes harsh regimes that deny the most basic human rights. Religions never accept universal human rights because their notion of rights derives from a higher revealed truth...This may be the last chance to say so before emergency measures ban 'incitement to religious hatred'. To say that religion is dangerous nonsense is indeed intended to incite people against

irrational superstition in favour of reason. But this law will insulate religious ideas in a sanctuary beyond scrutiny, refutation or ridicule. Why does religion deserve a realm beyond questioning?

...Religion must not be placed beyond criticism by accusations of Islamophobia, which has become a code for racism.

Polly Toynbee, The Guardian, 5 October 2001

Denying you the right to speak

David Blunkett's ...new offence of incitement to religious hatred would immediately liberate Speaker's Corner from the inciters who have been hogging it for hundreds of years ... Before long, the more bad-tempered or heated discussion programmes such as the Moral Maze or Question Time... will have to mend their ways, or disappear... In parts of Bradford, there must be great rejoicing over Blunkett's updating of Voltaire's defend-to-the-death doctrine, which might be summarised as follows: 'I don't know whether I agree with you or not, as I have devised a law denying you the right to speak.'

Catherine Bennett, The Guardian, 18 October 2001

---

sense of corporate belonging. Northern Ireland and parts of Scotland provide obvious examples within the United Kingdom. When this is the case, individuals are free to disown or disavow the tradition to which they belong only if (a) they are happy to be cut off from the community into which they have been born and which has nurtured their sense of identity and personal significance and (b) there is an alternative community which will fully welcome them and give them a sense of belonging.

It is rare for individuals to be happy to sever connections with their family and community, and equally rare for alternative families and communities to be genuinely available. Even if they do leave their tradition, individuals may still be perceived and labelled by others as belonging to their original roots, and may as a consequence be victims of discrimination, harassment and violence. The BNP leaflets quoted above, for example, were attacking people for their affiliation or presumed affiliation, not for their beliefs or observance. Affiliation, to repeat, is not always a matter of personal choice. It has some of the same qualities as ethnicity and so-called race.[5]

An attempt to sort the law out

In the House of Lords in 2002/03, Viscount Colville of Culross chaired an *ad hoc* select committee considering proposals for the scrapping of the blasphemy laws and their replacement with an offence of incitement to religious hatred. It began work in May 2002, following the demise of a Religious Offences Bill proposed by the Liberal Democrat peer Lord Avebury. The committee considered representations from Muslim organisations who said the blasphemy laws should not be scrapped but should instead be extended to cover other religions. This view met scepticism in the Upper House. As it was being convened, the peer Lord Peston sought assurances that it would be even handed so that 'those who regard the concept of a religious offence as nonsense will be represented' (Hansard: 15 May, 2002).

In the event, the committee – which reported on 10 June 2003 – took the view that greater protection is necessary for all faiths, but could not decide on what specific form it should take. Its report said: 'We support the protection of everyone's right to freedom of thought, conscience and religion, and the freedom

to manifest one's religion or beliefs, under Article 9 of the European Convention on Human Rights, and we consider that the ordinary law gives that protection. We agree however that there is a gap in the law as it stands. We have examined whether there needs to be any additional protection either for believers as a class, or for the objects connected with their beliefs. There is no consensus as to whether such protections should exist and, if so, the precise forms they should take, but we do agree that the civil and criminal law should afford the same protection to people of all faiths, and of none.' It appeared that the ball, once again, was in the government's court. The ruling outlined in Box 16 however, showed that substantial protection does in fact exist.

Policing and anti-terrorism

Research for the European Commission in 2003 reported that a high proportion of British Muslims perceive the police service to be racist.[6] There were references to disproportionate use of stop and search powers, discrimination in responding to calls, harassment of Muslims, 'macho, nationalistic and colonial' attitudes, and the failure of the service to recruit and retain Muslims. The accumulation of complaints and grievances meant that there is growing mistrust between the police and Muslim communities. In short, the criticisms and concerns were very similar to those which were discussed in the Stephen Lawrence Inquiry report. The recommendations made by the Lawrence report for combating racism in the police service are relevant also to combating Islamophobia. However, the distinctive features of Islamophobia need to be recognised.

The Anti Terrorism, Crime and Security Act (ATCSA) allows the Home Secretary powers to detain terrorist suspects, if they are not UK nationals, without arrest, charge, trial or any of the normal safeguards, for an unlimited period of time. In the words of Amnesty International, it 'effectively allows non-nationals to be treated as if they have been charged with a criminal offence, convicted without a trial and sentenced to an open-ended term of imprisonment'.[7]

The government had to opt out of Article 5 of the European Convention on Human Rights to assume those powers. As many feared, the legislation has been used to detain Muslims regarded by the security services as terrorist 'suspects'. Within a week of the Act being passed suspects were rounded up. Amnesty International attacked the detention as 'cruel' and in a paper for the Islamic Human Rights Commission the solicitor Natalia Garcia, who represented two of the men, reported that her clients were held in 'inhuman and degrading' conditions, locked up for 22 hours a day. She said of the legislation: 'So far it has only been used against Muslims. 'It is clearly the manifestation of state Islamophobia at its highest.' Following an appeal, the Special Immigration Appeals Commission broadly agreed. It found the detentions

---

Box 17

Where is your God now?
Police harassment of Muslims (*The Guardian,* December 2003)

Allegations surrounding one particular raid on December 2 appear to have brought matters to a head. In that case officers are alleged to have been responsible for a series of unprovoked attacks and to have subjected a suspect to Islamophobic abuse. Massoud Shadjareh, the chairman of the Islamic Human Rights Commission, said: 'The police force is behaving more like a vigilante force. Organisations have come together to say enough is enough.' Aafreen Khan, a spokeswoman for the Muslim Public Affairs Committee, added: 'Out of 500 arrests since September 11, only 77 have been charged and two convicted. That leaves 400-odd British Muslims who, through no fault of their own, have had their lives ruined with loss of jobs and local harassment. We are wondering whose son and husband will be next.'

Many Muslims cite the case of suspect A, who was one of four men arrested during a series of early morning raids, as highly symbolic. Yesterday he told *The Guardian* how his ordeal began as he and his wife were awakened by a loud bang. As six or seven officers burst into the room, the 29-year-old said he merely held his arms aloft. 'They were punching me in the head, on the back and on the legs. I must have taken about 30 strikes.' He said he had been pulled to the floor and only then did the officers seek to confirm his name. 'They told me I was being arrested under the Terrorism Act. I was completely shocked.'

He claims that as his wife was handcuffed the beating continued. One officer had grabbed his genitals and others swung his arms behind his back to handcuff him.

The suspect had never been arrested and said he initially thought the approach was normal. But then, it is claimed, the officers began mocking his beliefs. In a room set aside for prayer they allegedly broke candlestick holders. 'They put me in the prostrate position we adopt when we pray,' he said. 'They started laughing and asking, 'Where is your God now?'... I realised this was not an ordinary arrest.'

He says the laughing continued as the officers pulled down his leggings to search him. He was then pulled outside to the van where he claims the mistreatment continued. 'They laid me face down. One officer stood on my ankle and I took five or 10 punches to the back and kidneys. They were pulling and twisting the cuffs.

'Then, a few minutes into the journey, one guy put me into a headlock and squeezed until I was gasping for breath. He said, 'You will remember this day for the rest of your life you fucking bastard'.'

He claims the abuse continued until he was in the police station. Three days later, when a doctor was sent to examine him in the presence of a police doctor, he was found to have injuries to his face, scalp, neck, chest, back, upper arm, elbow, forearm, abdomen, thigh and both feet. Tests found blood in his urine.

He and three other men arrested during the operation were released without charge after seven days.

His solicitor, Muddassar Arani, said he had received no apology and personal effects taken during the raid had not been returned. 'This sort of behaviour is alienating Muslim communities,' she said. 'We hear a lot about these arrests but very little when these men are released, and nothing about the effect this has on their families.'

A Scotland Yard spokesman confirmed it had received a complaint but said no officer had been suspended. The case is expected to be referred to the Police Complaints Authority.

Source: from a news report by Hugh Muir, The Guardian, 13 December 2003. There is fuller information at www.incb.org.uk

---

were discriminatory and broke the European Convention on Human Rights. But the government appealed that decision and won. The status quo was re-established.

There is also mounting concern in Muslim communities about the impact of anti-terrorism legislation on UK nationals. The extract from a news item in December 2003 shown in Box 17 illustrates the concern and the kinds of report that are circulating. It shows also an example of alleged Islamophobic behaviour by a police officer. The statistical facts behind such reports and stories were published by the Home Office on 12 December 2003 and are as follows: In 2002-03 there were 32,100 searches under the Anti-Terrorism Act, 21,900 more than in the previous year and more than 30,000 above 1999-2000 levels. Resulting from the 32,100 searches, just 380 people were arrested.[8]

Sentencing

'The police have done a really good job in following this through and at last the courts are handing out sentences that are a genuine reprisal but also a message to the community.' That was David Blunkett's reaction when the young men involved in the Bradford riots of 2001 were brought to book. Those who complained that excessive sentences were handed out to the young Muslims – whom the Home Secretary described as 'maniacs' – were ordered to stop 'whining'. In February 2003 the Court of Appeal agreed with the Home Secretary. Despite the claims of campaigners who contended that the sentences of up to five years on riot charges were disproportionately heavier than those received by white youths and were an example of 'anti-Muslim paranoia', the Appeal Court judges ruled that the sentences were broadly right. They conceded that the Bradford Recorder Judge Gullick had erred in one regard. He said he was 'not concerned with the origins of the violence', a comment Lord Justice Rose called unfortunate, adding: 'If he meant that the origins were irrelevant, he was wrong.'[9]

The appeal judges reduced the sentences given to four of the twelve defendants before them, citing special mitigating circumstances which had not been sufficiently taken into account. But in all other respects they considered that justice had been done.

However, this was not the view of campaigners, who still believe the sentences handed down to young Muslims in Bradford and following disturbances in Leeds were disproportionate. According to an analysis conducted by the Institute of Race Relations, there was a huge discrepancy in the sentences imposed against the Manningham rioters, most of whom are of Pakistani heritage, and the sentences which have resulted from other cases of civil disturbance in the UK, including flashpoint areas such as Northern Ireland.

The analysis showed they were also out of kilter when compared to sentences given to people who rioted on a neighbouring, mostly white, estate the following day. After looking at 58 cases the IRR said it was concerned that the sentencing policy was not designed to reflect 'the severity of each individual's actions.' but sought instead to 'discipline an entire community'. Certainly the perception persists that the sentencing was unfair.

Prisons

In 1991 there were 731 Muslims in British prisons.[10] By 30 September 2003 there were 6095 and almost nine per cent of all prisoners were Muslims, compared with three per cent of Muslims in the general population. The factors underlying this growth are various. They include an increase in the number of Muslims amongst the section of the population most likely to be sentenced to prison, namely young males living in deprived areas; an increase in criminality, particularly in relations to drugs, amongst young Muslim men; an increase in the numbers of prisoners asserting their Muslim identity; and an increase in non-UK nationals in prison. There may also be, as widely suspected in Muslim communities, an increase in discrimination by the police service, the Crown Prosecution Service and the courts. Research is needed to establish the relative weight of these factors.

Whatever their relative weight there is clear evidence of racism in the prison service. The CRE found fourteen areas needing urgent action: the general atmosphere in prisons; treatment of prison staff; treatment of prisoners; access to goods, facilities and services; control of the use of discretion; prison transfers and allocations; discipline for prisoners; incentives and earned privileges; access to work; race complaints by prisoners; investigation of race complaints; correcting bad practice and spreading good practice; protection from victimisation; and management systems and procedures.[11] The cumulative effect of failings in all or most of these areas was the murder in his cell of a young British Muslim, Zahid Mubarek.

At much the same time that the CRE published its full report on racism in the prison service, a report was published by an academic who had himself been a prison governor.[12] He interviewed 45 young men, all of them black or Asian, in youth offender institutions. They reported that officers routinely used terms such as 'chimp' and 'golliwog' when addressing them. One had been told by an officer: 'You're a piece of shit. When I wipe my arse, it looks like you.' Racism based on appearance was mixed with racism based on religion and culture. The interviews were conducted at the height of the debate over whether Britain should go to war in Iraq and several of the Muslim inmates described how the racism they had to endure from officers was mixed with crude Islamophobia. 'We're bombing your country,' said an officer to a young British citizen of South Asian background. 'We're sending missiles over to bomb you to smithereens.'

The researcher read each of the institutions' most recent reports by the chief inspector of prisons before he visited. None of the prisons was seen as having any problems with racism, for key performance targets in relation to race had been achieved. 'The reports gave every single one of those establishments a clean bill of health as far as race was concerned,' he observed. 'There was this confidence in the procedures and bureaucracy of monitoring and managing race.' But the system described in the reports was, as it were, a virtual system, existing on paper and in observance of bureaucratic procedures, not in reality. 'None of it,' he said, 'related to these gross examples of simple, old-fashioned, direct, in your face 'when I wipe my arse the shit looks like you' racism.'[13]

Disparities between sound paperwork on the one hand and crude racism on the other will have to be addressed by the prison service. It will be crucial, in the long task ahead, to name and attend to Islamophobia. It cannot and must not be assumed that Islamophobia will automatically be dealt with if other forms of racism are dealt with. Within this context,

there are issues to do with the religious and cultural needs of Muslim prisoners. Such issues include the following:[14]

The timing of Friday noon prayers: many establishments claim that they are now doing their best to accommodate correct timings. Information on Friday prayers is in the new PSO 4550 on religion to be implemented by all prisons by April 2004.

Appointment of imams: ministers from any faith tradition need to be employed, on the basis of the needs of the prison. All chaplaincy teams need to review their resources and the distribution of resources between faiths, and to produce action plans in order to ensure that the distribution is appropriate and equitable.

Induction training for imams and chaplains: appropriate certificated training, using a mix of distance-learning and residential events, needs to be developed. In addition a multi-faith and inclusive handbook for chaplains, imams and visiting ministers has been issued and a programme of joint national and regional conferences is to be developed.

Halal food and hygiene: progress is being made on ensuring that dietary needs are properly observed, and requirements relating to hygiene and showering.

Sacred space: there are increasing examples of good practice in the provision of space for prayer and worship, used by members of all faiths.

Festivals: at Eid-al-Fitr and Eid-al-Adha Muslims should have the day off from work or education and arrangements should be made for congregational prayers from sunrise till noon, led by an imam.

In 2003 the Home Office indicated that it would like the probation service to work more closely with the voluntary and community sector in providing support and supervision for low-risk offenders, both pre-sentence and post-sentence, and in ensuring rehabilitation after sentences have been served. It is hoped and intended that Muslim organisations should be involved in this programme.

7. EMPLOYMENT AND SERVICES
Ensuring equality, responding to diversity

Summary

This chapter begins by pointing out that unemployment levels amongst people of Pakistani and Bangladeshi heritage in Britain are extremely serious and that the situation is worsening. It cites a major Cabinet Office study and reports on the new policies the government is adopting to remedy the situation. It notes that government policy appears nevertheless to be insensitive to issues of religious identity. Discrimination on grounds of religion or belief is now unlawful and in this connection the concepts of 'reasonable adjustment' and 'reasonable accommodation' are to be welcomed. These concepts are relevant also to issues of service delivery and the chapter concludes by giving some examples.

Discrimination and job prospects

A major report by the Cabinet Office in 2003 noted that employment rates amongst people of Pakistani and Bangladeshi heritage, as also amongst people of African-Caribbean heritage, are lower than those of the rest of the population. In addition, earnings and progression at work are persistently lower. Critically, these gaps are not closing.

'There is strong evidence,' said the report, 'that discrimination plays a significant role.' Equal opportunities legislation has had some success in combating overt discrimination and harassment, it noted, but 'indirect discrimination, where policies or practices have the inadvertent result of systematically disadvantaging ethnic minorities, remains a problem'.

The report proposed a wide range of measures to combat and reduce discrimination in recruitment and promotion policies, and in organisational cultures. In making these recommendations it acknowledged that race relations legislation and the Commission for Racial Equality have been important and valuable. It stressed also, however, that far more needs to be done if discrimination is to be significantly reduced.

The report was not principally about reducing discrimination. More especially, it was about increasing employability by raising levels of educational attainment and skills; connecting people of minority ethnic backgrounds with work by reforming existing employment programmes; tackling specific barriers to work in deprived areas, for example poor transport; and promoting and supporting self employment. Further, it was concerned with structures to ensure that real changes and improvements take place. For example, action on delivery will be led by a minister in charge of a cross-departmental task force comprising relevant ministers, senior officials and key external stakeholders. The task force will report through the secretary of state for work and pensions to the cabinet committee on economic affairs, productivity and competitiveness.

The report was impressive in the quality of its data; in its seriousness; and in the number and likely consequences of its practical recommendations. However, its chapter on equal opportunities contained no reference to discrimination on grounds of religion or belief, other than in an incidental quotation from the Human Rights Act. Equally seriously, there was no indication that the new government strategies and programmes to improve employability and job opportunities will need to be sensitive and responsive to religious needs and outlooks.

Throughout, the report's concern was with 'ethnic minorities'. It mentioned that where 'greater precision is required with reference to specific component groups within the ethnic minority population, allowances and departures from this term are made in the text'. This meant, for example, that there were occasional references in the text to Pakistani and Bangladeshi communities, It did not, however, mean that there was any reference to religious identity.

The report made next to no reference to racism and none at all to Islamophobia. A critique of it in *The*

Muslim News pointed out 'that the current media reportage and public discourse on Islam and Muslims have a huge impact on Muslim labour market performance. The impact begins to bite at a very early age in the life of a Muslim child. It affects how Muslim children are treated in schools by staff and other pupils, it affects the self-esteem of Muslim children, and all this affects their educational achievement. Beyond education, its impact bites at each and every stage of British Muslim adult life.'[1] The article noted that the advisory group for the report had had 29 members but that not one was a Muslim. Yet Muslims constitute 35 per cent of the people whose life chances the report claimed to be considering. The absence of Muslims on the group, as also the invisibility of Muslims in the report itself, was a striking example of institutional Islamophobia.

A recent change

For many years non-governmental organisations (NGOs) in the UK, both Muslim and non-Muslim, complained regularly to the United Nations Committee on Eliminating Racial Discrimination (CERD) about the failure of the UK government to make discrimination on religious grounds unlawful in Great Britain. In 1992, 1996 and 2000 the committee agreed formally with the criticism and on each occasion delivered a strong rebuke. The official response from the UK was a mantra-type protest that such legislation would be impossible, for (so it was claimed) it would require making a legal distinction between a religion and a cult.[2] But in due course, as a result of legislative change at European level, the UK government conceded that it had no choice but to accept the criticism and, in effect, that its claims about the prior need to define the difference between a religion and a cult had been ill-founded.

The European Directive of 2000/78/EC 27 November 2000 under Article 13 of the European Union Treaty has been incorporated into British domestic legislation and has been in force since December 2003.[3] It is one of the most important pieces of legislation for faith communities across the continent, for it will provide substantial protection against cases of religious discrimination in employment. It will allow claims to be bought by Muslim women, for example, who are subjected to harassment or abuse because of their

dress at the workplace. Employment practices which fail to accommodate time off for employees to observe religious holidays or events could also be challenged at last.

In the UK, the anomaly remains that legislation with similar intentions and effects has been on the statute book in Northern Ireland for many years. Religious affiliation, in the sense of community belonging, is seen both as a significant aspect of someone's identity and as a factor that can cause unfair discrimination. The Fair Employment and Treatment (Northern Ireland) Order 1998 (FETO) prohibits direct discrimination in employment on the grounds of religious belief[a] or political opinion and places a range of specific duties on employers. All employers with more than ten full-time employees are required to register with the Fair Employment Commission, and to submit an annual report to the commission providing details of the community background of their workforce in terms of employees' affiliation with the Protestant or the Roman Catholic communities. They must review their recruitment, training and promotion practices at least once every three years in order to determine whether fair participation in employment is being secured for both Protestants and Roman Catholics.

In Great Britain, the new legislation will have an impact not only on recruitment procedures but also on workplace routines and culture. A key concept in this regard will be 'reasonable adjustment'. There are further notes about this below.

Adjustment and accommodation

The terms 'reasonable adjustment' and 'reasonable accommodation' are well known in the UK in connection with disability discrimination. In other English-speaking countries, however, particularly Canada, they are used in connection with the whole range of equal opportunities issues, not just disability issues. For example, they include religion. They are likely to become increasingly well known in UK workplaces from 2004 onwards, following the implementation of the EU Employment Directive.

'Accommodation' is the customary term in Canada and the United States, and 'adjustment' in Australia and the UK. Both terms have their advantages, though neither is ideal. Although the actual terms are unfamiliar to most people in the UK at present, the actual concepts have been around for centuries – at all times and in all places human beings make adjustments to their practices, customs and policies in order to accommodate different interests, needs and concerns. They typically do this through processes of discussion, negotiation and compromise – namely through reasoning with each other in a spirit of good will rather than through coercion and brute power. The root syllable of the word accommodation appears also in 'moderate' and 'modest': the concern is to devise systems that are *good enough*, not totally perfect and not making a great fuss or drawing attention to themselves.

In relation to religion in UK workplaces, there are already many examples of reasonable adjustment. The Employment Directive will strengthen and spread good practice that already exists. It is worth spelling out that good practice has three aspects: processes of discussion to find mutually satisfactory solutions; the making of adjustments; the acceptance of what is reasonable, as distinct from what is ideal. The issues which arise with religion in the workplace include the following:

- time off for festivals and holy days
- time off for attendance at worship
- facilities for prayer at the workplace itself
- uniform and dress codes
- menus and procedures in staff canteens
- the visual environment
- the norms of occupational culture

Employers and managers will need to be guided by general principles, in the first instance, not by rules.[5] Such principles will be clarified through the discussion of real or imaginary cases such as those shown in Box 18.

It is relevant to recall that adjustments made under the Disability Discrimination Act are often useful not only for people who are registered as disabled but for others as well – ramps, for example, are useful for wheelchairs but also for adults with infant children, and for adults with heavy luggage equipped with wheels, and for anyone with a temporary injury. Similarly, adjustments to cater for religious needs are often directly useful for a wide range of people. Indirectly, deliberations about what is reasonable (see

---

Box 18

What is reasonable?
some situations and scenarios

A secretary currently employed by a church organisation converts to Islam. Is it reasonable for her to insist on wearing hijab when at work? Is it reasonable for the employer to demand that she does not, and to dismiss her if she refuses to comply?

A peripatetic teacher teaches on Fridays at a certain school. He wishes to attend prayers at his mosque, which happens to be an hour's journey away. So if he attends mosque he misses half a day's work. Is this reasonable?

A member of a certain Christian denomination refuses on religious grounds to use computers at her place of employment. Is this reasonable?

A member of staff at a hotel becomes an observant Jew. He refuses to work on Friday evenings and all day Saturday. Is it reasonable for the hotel manager to dismiss him?

Muslim staff at a certain workplace request that a prayer room be provided during Ramadan. Is this reasonable? Is it reasonable for management to refuse the request, on the grounds that it cannot be afforded?

At his annual appraisal interview a young executive is advised that if he really wishes to achieve promotion he ought to go to the pub with colleagues, in order to mix informally and socially. On religious grounds, he does not consume alcohol. Is the advice reasonable? Is it reasonable for him to make a formal complaint?

Box 18) are likely to benefit all employees in an organisation, not just those who have strong religious affiliation[5].

Provision of services

It is anomalous and deeply unsatisfactory that reasonable adjustments in relation to religion or belief are required by law in employment matters but not in service delivery matters. The new legal requirements on employment are likely, however, to have an indirect influence on service delivery, since the same principles of reasonable adjustment are relevant. This was tacitly recognised by the CRE in official guidance relating to the implementation of the Race Relations (Amendment) Act. Some examples of good practice cited by the CRE are reprinted in Box 19. One is about reasonable adjustment in an employment matter. The other three show entirely clearly that the CRE envisages situations where the promotion of race equality requires recognition of religious diversity and identity. However, the Code and the non-statutory guidance could and should have made this point explicitly, not left it to be implied through random examples.

The essential theoretical point illustrated in Box 19 is that organisations need to be discriminating without at the same time being discriminatory. For it is as unjust to treat people similarly when in relevant respects they are different as it is to treat them differently when in relevant respects they are alike. This is particularly obvious in matters relating to gender and disability – it can be unjust to treat women as if in all respects their life-experiences, needs and interests are the same as those of men, and vice versa, and it can be unjust not to make reasonable adjustments and accommodations to take account of the needs of people with disabilities. In the fields of inter-ethnic, inter-cultural and inter-racial relationships, it is similarly unjust to be 'colour-blind' or 'difference-blind', for not all people have the same narratives, life-experiences, perceptions and frames of reference. The distinctive experiences and frames of reference of Muslims, for example, must be recognised. Such recognition is required not only in the workplace but

---

Box 19

Special sessions
Examples of reasonable adjustment

Leisure service programmes for Muslim women

Every year, a leisure service surveys the people who use its leisure centres. The leisure centres are in a multicultural area, with large Pakistani Muslim and Somali Muslim populations. The most recent surveys showed that almost none of these women used the centres. The service had never thought of running special sessions for women, but after discussing the survey results with local ethnic minority community groups, the service has introduced special sessions for Pakistani and Somali women. It has co-operated with local voluntary groups that work with Pakistani and Somali communities, and it is now including sessions within a 'healthy living' education programme for Muslim women.

A police service modifies dress code requirements

For many years, a police service has been actively following an equal opportunities policy in employment. Women from Muslim communities, however, are seriously under-represented in the force. The police service has therefore introduced a new version of the uniform for female officers which allows them to wear a headscarf. The force hopes that this will encourage more Muslim women to join.

Modified appointments scheme for out-patients

An NHS Trust out-patients department reviewed the appointments not kept by patients. An analysis of the missed appointments showed that a disproportionately high number of ethnic minorities did not attend on certain days. Further analysis showed that many of these failed appointments were on holy days or festivals (for example during Eid, Greek Easter, Diwali, St Patrick's Day). As a result, the out-patients department placed a multi-faith and multi-ethnic calendar on the computer system and appointments staff were then alerted to these days so that they could avoid them when making certain appointments.

Adjustments to an options scheme

An art department monitored applications by subject and found that Asian students – mainly those of Pakistani background – were well represented on all courses except the fine arts course. A survey of Muslim students found that they were interested in some of the other fine art modules. The department responded by reviewing its course options, and made sure that fine art modules were available as options to students on other courses.

---

also in the planning, provision and delivery of services.

Box 20 contains reflections by a clinical psychologist on principles of reasonable adjustment within his own sphere of professional concern, that of counselling people who are mentally ill. The reflections were made in the context of a lecture at a conference and were offered as a basis for discussion not as formal or official recommendations. Broadly similar reflections are relevant in a wide range of other services also.

One of the most significant examples in recent years of reasonable adjustment in the provision of services took place in the banking system. Under Islamic law, the receipt and payment of interest is forbidden and many Muslims are reluctant to take out mortgages from banks and building societies to finance home purchase. In response to this need, a working party was established by the Bank of England and in his April 2003 Budget the Chancellor introduced a measure (abolition of double stamp duty) that has opened the way for financial institutions such as HSBC to offer home purchasing schemes to Muslims in accordance with Islamic law.

In a speech in February 2003 to the Council of Mortgage Lenders, the Governor of the Bank of England, Sir Eddie George, congratulated members on the progress they had made on the question of Islamic mortgages and noted that it would be not only a useful business opportunity for companies involved in the provision of housing finance but also a welcome diversification of the UK's financial system more generally. Further, it would:

> demonstrate in a small, but significant and very practical, way a commitment on the part of the authorities in this country, working together with the private sector, financial and professional community and with representatives of our ethnic minority population – in this case our Muslim population – to accommodate differences of religious principle or tradition insofar as we can without in any way undermining the values or traditions of our indigenous society.

Concluding note

Ideally, what is now required is a single Equality Act. This was argued in scholarly detail by Professor

---

Box 20

More sensitive ways
Proposals for mental health services

If one is to make mental health services more culturally sensitive in ways that improve outcome, how does one go about it? I suggest:

Allow, as far as is practicable, a physical environment in which clients can feel culturally unstressed, particularly over matters of spiritual or religious practice, as religion is often the pivot of culture.

This includes provision of single sex wards, prayer facilities, appropriate diet, not being gung-ho at getting patients to join in other people's cultural festivals, and allowing Feng Shui devotees to arrange their private space as they wish.

Not actively seeking to deculturalise clients as part of therapy. It may seem that such so clearly represents bad practice that it need not even be mentioned. However, to give just one example, it was recently the practice at my own hospital to deliberately put Asian patients in gender-mixed therapy groups, in order to break down cultural 'inhibitions'. There was never any evidence presented to suggest this practice had the slightest therapeutic value.

As a general rule, not to undermine clients' (and their families') own concepts of mental illness. This is not to say that over-valued ideas or delusions cannot be challenged – delusions are by definition ideas that are inappropriate to a person's own cultural background. It may, however, mean that one does not seek to disabuse a patient from their belief that their mental disorder is caused by spirit possession, or an imbalance in the body's humours, or the doubtful quality of the local water supply. It is quite possible to advance an alternative model without contradicting the patient's own beliefs.

The above three suggestions are essentially about modifying clinical culture within the present NHS system. They do not have large resource implications and they do not involve a wholesale re-think of the way NHS services are provided. My final point may do.

Therapies should be on offer in the NHS which match the cultures of different client groups.

Source: lecture by Rasjid Skinner, Harrogate, 2001

Hepple and his colleagues at the University of Cambridge in a report published in 2000. It was also argued in the report of the Commission on Multi-Ethnic Britain, published a few months later. A bill on the subject was presented by Lord Lester of Herne Hill to the House of Lords in May 2003. The government is not at present minded to introduce such legislation, so inconsistencies and anomalies will remain. Eventually, almost certainly, a single act will be inevitable. By then, case law, common sense, good will and reasonable adjustments will perhaps have been such that the new law will endorse and codify existing practice rather than compel new practice.

If this admittedly utopian hope proves to be well founded, some of the credit will be due to developments in the education system, and in the educational activities that Muslim communities themselves organise. Education is the subject of the next chapter.

8. IDENTITY AND EDUCATION
Foundations of the future

Summary

This chapter begins with quotations from interviews with several teenagers, conducted especially for this report. The interviewees were all British Muslims and they describe vividly how they see themselves and their futures. Discussion follows about attainment, the curriculum, school ethos and organisation, dealing with Islamophobia in the playground, and debates around the place of Muslim schools within the state education system.

Recent experiences and possible futures

The teenagers quoted in Box 21 are all young women. They are proud of their Muslim identity and more aware of it since 9/11; wearing hijab, it is clear, is important for them, signalling both to themselves and to others who they are. They do not feel pressurised to wear hijab but on the contrary feel wholly free to make their own decisions. They have high hopes and aspirations but frequently feel unwelcome in British society and uncertain therefore about their personal future, not least because of the offensive Islamophobia they meet in their everyday lives in interaction with other students. Some of them are deeply critical of the UK government's foreign policy and for this reason too feel alienated and ill at ease. The fact that millions of non-Muslims opposed the war on Iraq, however, is a matter of much encouragement and moral support to them.

Next, some young men (Box 22). They have much the same concerns as the young women. They too are extremely critical of the media and of how Islam is represented. And there is a similar determination to assert their identity and to contribute to the building of a fairer Britain. They commend organisations such the Muslim Council of Britain but also seek and accept personal responsibility for making Islam better known and more respected.

The quotations in Boxes 21 and 22 from young British Muslims depict a generation that is torn between insecurity and confidence, anxiety and hope, doubt and determination.[1] The people quoted are clear that they wish to be seen as both British and Muslim and that they are resolved to ensure that their dual identity is recognised and respected. On balance, there is more hope and resolution amongst them than insecurity and doubt. In so far as these young people are typical, the future looks bright.

It would be misleading, however, to imply that there are no other kinds of voice and stance amongst young British Muslims. There are also those who feel disillusioned, rootless and alienated, and who do not feel that their identity in Britain is even tolerated, let alone welcomed. They are likely to engage in what a writer quoted in a later chapter (see Box 30) calls 'the violence of the violated', both to their own disadvantage and to that of others. It is from this group, also, that the rising numbers of young Muslims in prison mostly come.[2] Box 23 contains some descriptions of them written by observers.

Achievement

As mentioned in Box 23, the lack of educational achievement amongst some young British Muslims is a matter of great concern, as are the unemployment and alienation to which it leads. There is no national data cross-tabulating educational achievement with religious affiliation. Since summer 2003, however, there is national data on the educational achievement of the two thirds of Muslims who have origins in Pakistan or Bangladesh.[3] It shows:

Box 21

Proud

Voices of Muslim school students – (a) young women

'I am proud to be a British Muslim. I didn't used to wear a scarf. But now I follow my custom to show how proud I am of my religion. We have free will to understand our own religion, it's not as though we are forced to wear the scarf. Women have a lot of freedom within Islam. The headscarf is just about protecting yourself. Men are less likely to be tempted if you are covered up.' *Hina, 16*

'People used to ask me why I wear my headscarf. People used to say I looked nicer without it, so I took it off because I was a bit embarrassed. But now I'm in Year Nine and I'm becoming more of a lady I want to wear it. Some people think we are forced to wear them but my parents don't mind either way. It was my choice.' *Mariam, 14*

'The way people talk about Muslims and Jihad makes us feel guilty, even though there are no reasons to feel like that. Sometimes people look at me and I imagine they're thinking 'go back to your own country'. After September 11 one black girl said to me, 'now you know how black people feel'... I went to visit a sixth form college in Havering with my mum. We were both wearing long skirts and headscarves. As we were walking around some of the girls were whispering and laughing at us. I know I want to do A levels and go to university and I thought I wanted to go to that college, but now I don't know where to go. I don't feel welcome. I am a bit lost. Where will I end up?' *Asma, 16*

'It's horrible when your own government is helping to kill Muslims. You just feel so helpless. Sometimes I feel ashamed to be British when I go abroad ... I have been called names. I was with a friend in East Ham once and we were both wearing scarves. An old man came up to us and shouted that we were 'bloody Muslims'. You just feel so angry and helpless.' *Fazeela, 15*

'Eid this year was the worst. You wake up and you are supposed to be happy and have a good day with your family, but you turn on the TV and you see soldiers guarding the airport. It just gives you a sinking feeling. It's pathetic... I do a lot of sport with a group of Asian girls and a couple of us wear headscarves. Once when we were playing another school one of the girls said look at all these Asians, they all look the same.' *Mumtal, 14*

'I used to call myself British Muslim but when they started bombing Afghanistan I didn't want to be British any more ... But seeing all those people marching really helped. First you believe that they are against Muslims, but when you see that amount of support for the people of Iraq it makes you strong.' *Zainab, 14*

Source: interviews in summer 2003 by Laura Smith

- Compared with the national average of 51 per cent, 45 per cent of students of Bangladeshi heritage achieved five A*-C passes in summer 2001 and 40 per cent of students of Pakistani heritage.

- This compared with 73 per cent of students of Chinese heritage, 64 per cent of students of Indian heritage (some of whom, incidentally, would be Muslims), 40 per cent of students of African heritages (and again, some of these would be Muslim) and 30 per cent of students of African-Caribbean heritage.

- In all communities there was a significant difference between girls' and boys' attainment. In the case of Pakistani communities, only 34 per cent of boys in Pakistani communities achieved five passes A*-C in 2002, compared with 48 per cent of girls.

Such figures have to be treated with great caution for two main reasons. First, there are huge differences between Pakistani communities in Britain with regard to class, occupation and migration history. Figures for the whole mask the distinctive sitation of Muslim young people in northern towns and cities. Second, such statistics do not compare like with like. In terms of social class, that is to say, the profile of the white

Box 22

We need to come out
Voices of Muslim school students – (b) young men

'It is upsetting when you see that all Muslims are tarred with the same brush. We are all Osama bin Ladens or something and we all want to kill everyone. And it's not true. Sometimes you get people looking at you funny. They assume that you are Muslim so you must be a terrorist ...For things to change people need to go out and portray the true Islam. Muslims always go into a corner and never come out to express their views. We need to come out and teach people about Islam. That's the only way people will recognise us and who we are. My parents' generation didn't have that opportunity, but we do.' *Farid, 15*

'People have a stereotyped view of Islam. They think Muslims are old fashioned and live in tents with camels. They see us as people who haven't moved with the times or technology. They compare people to the West – the way they dress, the way they live their lives, the way they work. And they see it as all old style. The main problem is that they don't know much about Islam... After September 11 the media wanted us to condemn this attack, as if it was our responsibility. The Muslim Council of Britain came out and condemned it but that wasn't enough. The MCB speak for us as a community so what more did they want? Did they want every single Muslim to issue a statement?' *Yasir, 16*

'The media only shows a negative view of Islam. On television, sometimes they show Muslims, but it's always them doing some sort of Islamic ritual or being extremists. They don't show us as normal people... If a reporter wants a nice big headline, an attractive front-page story, they aren't going to go to someone nice and peaceful. They will go to Abu Hamza and take his quotations and have a story about Islamic extremists. I think it is quite hard for them because they don't know about Islam, but sometimes it feels like a conscious decision.' *Othman, 16*

'One thing that September 11 did was start getting people more interested. People starting buying the Qur'an and being more open to learning about Islam. The marches as well showed that it wasn't just Muslims that opposed the war. There were a lot of English people there too. That was encouraging, even though I think we were marching for different reasons.' *Khaled, 16*

'They talk about democracy and then they put men in shackles at Guantanamo Bay. Where are the human rights? ... I don't agree with suicide bombings. But if you are a little boy and you see your parents killed in front of you; if you are a teenager and you see your little brother getting shot, you are going to grow up feeling angry. But people don't want to listen.' *Nael, 16*

Source: interviews in summer 2003 by Laura Smith

community is substantially different from that of the Pakistani community.[4] It is well known that educational attainment and social class are closely related.[5]

If under-achievement in some British Muslim communities is to be effectively tackled, there are several questions for investigation and action research. Such questions are listed in Box 24.

Muslim schools

In 1997, when the Commission's report was published, there were no state-funded Muslim schools. Since then, four Muslim schools have become state-funded.

The Islamia Primary School in Brent, London, became Britain's first state-funded Muslim school in 1998, and was followed by Al Furqan primary in Birmingham the same year, Feversham College secondary school in Bradford in September 2001 and Al Hijrah secondary in Birmingham in September 2002. A further school – Al-Risaala, in Balham, London – is to enter the state sector under a new name in September 2004 and plans have been approved for a school in Leicester.

There are currently about 120 Muslim schools in the UK, all of which – apart from those mentioned above – are funded by parents and the community. There are

Box 23

Everything we don't want our kids to be
Concerns about Muslim youth

Unemployed and poorly educated

We laugh along with Ali G because he is everything we do not wish our kids to be, yet see evidence of daily... The species of nominal Muslim Ali G is meant to represent [is] typically unemployed and poorly educated, he is the type who sees a brighter future in taking on the trappings of the LA 'gangsta' rather than the uncool and 'foreign' traditions of his parents. The sovereigns, the Tommy Hillfiger 'condom' hat, the goatee beard and the glasses all mark him out as that breed of young British Muslim whose idea of getting down has more to do with the dance floor than the prayer mat.... The character gives the lie to the sound bite that Islam is Britain's fastest growing religion...The British Muslim community is haemorrhaging. *Faisal Bodi, Q News, February 2000*

Assertive Muslim identity

Such research as exists into Muslim youth in London, Birmingham and Bradford allows us to draw certain tentative conclusions. First, among sections of youth there is the growth of an 'assertive Muslim identity' which can impact negatively on women. Secondly, this 'assertive Muslim identity' has to be distinguished from membership of self-consciously Islamic groups, which encompass the full range of Islamic expression, from quietist Sufi groups to strident radical groups. Thirdly, while cultural boundaries between youth are increasingly permeable, Muslim norms still limit interaction at many points with non-Muslim youth, especially for women. Fourthly, there is a general failure of traditional Muslim leadership, religious and political, to connect with the world of British Muslim youth. *Philip Lewis, University of Leeds, 2001*

Islam.... plays a role in the construction of masculinity ... a 'hard' image of tough aggressive macho men...[They claimed] membership of Hamas or Hizb-ut-Tahrir... yet were unaware who Shias were, and how they differed from Sunnis, and did not know what Hamas or Hizb-ut-Tahrir represent. Neither were they observant in their religious rituals...and were quite often in trouble with the police for petty crime, drugs etc. Thus the daubing of the walls ... with the slogan 'Hamas Rules OK' , or supporting antisemitic, homophobic and misogynist organisations such as Hizb-ut-Tahrir, was more an act of rebellion and defiance rather than the rise of 'fundamentalism'. It is all about being 'hard'... These affiliations seemed to be linked with territory...with Islamic nomenclature, such as Hamas, Hizb-ut-Tahrir or Tablighi Jamaat used to map and define territorial control. *Yunas Samad 1998*

We need to be scared

Pressure from the authorities, combined with the sentiments of most congregations, have pushed many young extremists out of the mosques. They have had to find new venues to socialise. These have been out of the scrutiny of the community. Nobody has a clue about what kind of theology these young Muslims are developing. But informed more by rage than the message of peace within traditional Islam, the results are likely to be dangerous. This does not augur well for either community relations or for the development of Islam in Britain. In their dark underground world, these young angry people have, like our government, lost their sense of what is legal, moral or humane. When two million anti-war demonstrators cannot stop the war, the message to these young people is clear. We need to be scared, very scared. The end of the war in Iraq might usher in the beginning of our own intifada. *Fuad Nahdi, 2003*

about 750,000 Muslim children in the UK. About one per cent attend Muslim schools and 0.5 per cent are in non-Muslim private schools. The vast majority are in the mainstream state sector.

The community cohesion reports into the disorders in northern cities in summer 2001, together with the Ouseley report on Bradford, have not helped key debates, for they implied or claimed that Muslim schools would be unacceptably divisive.[6] Also they muddied the issues by failing to distinguish between state schools that are secular in their ethos but happen to have high numbers of Muslim pupils as against voluntary-aided schools that are formally committed to Islamic values and which aim to provide an Islamic

Box 24

Questions for research

Recognising British Muslim identity

Muslim pupils experience a range of demands and expectations – from parents, community, the mosque, the school, their peers. How do schools help their pupils, both in the curriculum and in the pastoral system, to balance the pressures on them and to develop their identity?

Partnership with parents, mosques and community organisations

Some schools and LEAs have good working relationships with Muslim parents and organisations. Others, however, frankly admit that there is much progress still to be made. What are the key success factors here, and what seem to be the problems and obstacles that have to be overcome? What effect does partnership have on pupils' attainment? What is the role of governors?

Working with madrassas

High proportions of Muslim pupils attend classes at their local mosque. There is great potential for close cooperation between mosques and schools, so that the children's educational experience is holistic, and such that school and madrassas complement each other. How can this closer cooperation be encouraged, organised and supported?

Preventing and addressing racism and Islamophobia

It is widely recognised that institutional racism, as described and discussed in chapter 6 of the Stephen Lawrence Inquiry report, is likely to be a factor in the under-achievement of ethnic minority pupils. Racism takes a variety of forms, however, and in the case of Muslim pupils account must be taken of the form of racism known as Islamophobia. What are schools doing about this?

The international situation

The views of both Muslims and non-Muslims in Britain about Islam and Muslim identity are affected by events and developments overseas. The war in Iraq is the most recent example. It is also relevant to recall others, including the situation in Israel/ Palestine; Al Qaida and the 'war on terror'; and the situation in Gujarat State, India. How do schools manage the tensions and practical problems?

Multilingualism, language policy and English as an additional language

The DfES refers to two main groups of under-achieving pupils: those of African-Caribbean heritage and those who are bilingual. The implication is that difficulties faced by Muslim pupils are to do essentially with language and bilingualism. How can difficulties connected with language and other kinds of difficulty be separated out?

Alienation and vicious circles

When young people experience failure at school they often turn for moral support to their peer-group, or more widely to youth culture and street culture. If the sub-culture to which they turn is anti-school, as it often is, there is increasing alienation, for there is then a vicious circle or spiral of mutual antagonism and rejection. In the case of Muslim pupils the sub-cultures to which they may turn include some which are characterised by the phenomena loosely grouped under the label as 'fundamentalism' or 'extremism'. The phenomena include a substantial and possibly violent rejection, allegedly in the name of Islam, of all things western. How do schools respond to this?

Religion and faith in secular society

The presence of observant Muslim communities in secular European societies raises many complex issues of political philosophy, for example to do with the nature of pluralism, the limits of tolerance and dissent, the nature of truth claims, the interplay of public and private spheres, the politics of recognition and presence, the rules of debate, and the management of disagreement. How should such issues feature in continuing professional development, particularly management training for headteachers and other senior staff?

Differentials in attainment between boys and girls

There appears to be an emerging pattern, in many but not all LEAs, that boys of Pakistani and Kashmiri heritage have lower attainment than girls of the same heritage, and than of boys of other ethnicities. What are the factors causing or contributing to this? What is the role of teenage youth culture? What have schools successfully done to combat and reverse the trend?

Source: the RAISE Project 2003, funded by Yorkshire Forward

Box 25

Schools with Muslims and Muslim schools
– two case-studies

Case-study A: a school with Muslims

Plashet School is a multi-faith girls' comprehensive with more than 1,300 students. Nearly 90 per cent of the girls come from Asian families and over 90 per cent speak English as an additional language. There are high levels of poverty in the area and over half the students have a free meals entitlement. The majority of girls – 65 per cent – are Muslim, around ten per cent are Hindu and ten per cent Sikh.

Separate Muslim, Hindu, Sikh, Christian and multi-faith assemblies are held every week and girls can choose which they attend, whatever their religion. This has helped not only to give the girls a wide religious understanding, but also to forge links with local communities, who organise the assemblies and send speakers. Twelve of the 89 teachers are Muslim.

Issues such as sex education and swimming classes – potentially a point of conflict with parents – are dealt with sensitively. Rather than use the pool nearest the school, for example, a deal has been made with another further away which offers the school sole use for a few hours per week.

Plashet has achieved beacon status and most pupils go on to higher education. As well as being academically successful, the school places importance on the arts, music and sport.

Headteacher Mrs Nasir said: 'I am a Muslim and very committed to my religion. But because of my experience within education I am committed to the idea of multi-religious schools. One of the principles of school must be to prepare pupils for the outside world. If they are in segregated in school I think children actually miss out a great deal.' She added: 'Despite the mix I can honestly say we don't have problems here with bullying or name-calling. We do a lot in the school to try to ensure there is good cultural and religious understanding.'

Case study B: a Muslim school

Islamia School in Brent is a privately-funded secondary school for 125 girls aged 11 to 16. The school has a sixth form, but from September 2003 this was subsumed within the Islamic College of Advanced Education in north London.

Pupils of more than 20 nationalities attend the school. They originate from South Asia, the Middle East and Eastern Europe, and there is also a significant number of girls of mixed heritage. Many of the pupils come from financially constrained backgrounds. Of the 15 members of staff, three are non-Muslim, including a Christian and a Buddhist. The school has come first or second in the league tables in Brent for the last few years, and has repeatedly achieved a 100 per cent success rate in students attaining GCSE grades A* to C.

The school places great importance on the study of religions other than Islam and regularly organises functions with other schools and religious groups to learn about and debate other faiths. Sport, art and music are also valued, and the school has a choral group that performs locally. Basma Elshayyal, head of religious education, said: 'The faith aspect is really important. We try to achieve a holistic approach to the girls' lives rather than compartmentalising everything. The ethics and morals permeate the whole attitude of the school. So we teach the girls that they can be a citizen of the world and a positive contributor in every area of their lives – in the wider world, within their family, with different religious groups. This is very important because it helps to prevent the identity crisis which can be a symptom of being a minority. I know the girls appreciate it. It does improve their self-confidence.'

Source: interviews by Laura Smith, summer 2003

Box 26

What have Muslims ever done for us?
Islam Awareness Week 2003

Now in its ninth year, Islam Awareness Week is an opportunity for Muslims to communicate with the public at large and help to remove misunderstandings about Islam. In November 2002 the Islamic Society of Britain commissioned a public opinion survey by the respected pollsters YouGov to mark the beginning of Islam Awareness Week. The poll found that 74 per cent of respondents said that they knew 'nothing or next to nothing about Islam' and 64 per cent that their main source of information on Islam and Muslims was the media.

The theme for IAW in 2003 was Muslim heritage. The purpose was to challenge the notion that some hold about Islam being a religion of frustration, anger, violence and backwardness. It showed how Muslims have contributed to the lives of people around them and left a mark for centuries to come. By giving Muslim youth positive role models, the further purpose was to give them the confidence to believe in their heritage and faith and much needed inspiration to excel and contribute to modern day life.

During the week there were activities aimed at giving information about the Islamic way of life, promoting social interaction, celebrating art and culture and showing how Muslim history and heritage have contributed to the development of the modern world.

A new website (www.thevirtualclassroom.net) was launched from the House of Commons by the Secretary of State for Education, to help schools educate pupils about Muslim heritage in an enjoyable and exciting way.

There was a day of national fasting. People of many different faiths and backgrounds took part to show that our diverse communities can get together in an atmosphere of mutual understanding and for a good cause. We wanted to show that the true spirit of Islam is one of charity, kindness and feeling for one's community. The monies raised were shared between local charities; the Water and Sanitation Project run by Islamic Relief; the Healthcare Programme run by Muslim Aid); Cancer Research: and the Prince's Trust.

Source: adapted from information at www.iaw.org.uk

ethos. The issues have been further muddied by the misleading term 'monocultural schools' to describe state schools with high numbers of Muslim pupils.

Two case studies illustrate the differences and similarities between secular schools with large numbers of Muslim pupils and schools formally committed to Islamic values. These appear in Box 25.

Of nearly 7,000 state faith schools in England, 33 are Jewish, two are Sikh, one Greek Orthodox and one Seventh Day Adventist. The Jewish community in Britain numbers just under 260,000 and the Sikh community just under 330,000 – compared with a Muslim population of 1.6 million. The disparities between numbers in the population and numbers of faith-based schools in the state education system continues to be a source of great grievance.   .

Curriculum

The Stephen Lawrence Inquiry report recommended that the whole national curriculum should be reviewed to make it more antiracist and multicultural. The government accepted the recommendation but the only substantial measures it has taken to implement it have been the creation of two websites, the one at the QCA and the other managed by the DfES itself. The websites are useful and stimulating, but there is still much progress to be made. The three greatest needs are for:

- an overall framework of overarching concepts and issues that should be taught, as appropriate, across all subjects and at all age levels
- guidance on teaching about racism and Islamophobia
- guidance on teaching about Islam

With regard to the last of these, exemplary work has been done over the years in connection with Islamic Awareness Week, observed each year in November. The project is spearheaded by the Islamic Society of Britain but involves a range of other Muslim organisations as well, both nationally and at local levels. 'When I was in school,' remarked the national organiser in 2003, 'we learnt about Greeks and Romans – the usual 'what the Romans did for us' stuff. Nobody taught us how much Britain and Europe owe to Muslim civilisation. The modern world would be impossible without this Muslim contribution; it's a heritage we all share. It's the real antidote to the nonsense about a clash of civilizations. It's the best way to teach young Muslims they're part of this society – that they have a lot to live up to – to teach non-Muslims to appreciate them in a new, positive way.' There is information about the 2003 programme in Box 26.

In addition to teaching about Islam, as outlined in Box 26, consideration needs to be given to the wider inclusion of Arabic within the framework of modern foreign languages, and to the inclusion of issues of Islamophobia and British Muslim identity in the citizenship curriculum.

Ethos and organisation

The 1997 report on Islamophobia urged that written guidelines should be published by central government on meeting the pastoral, religious and cultural needs of Muslim pupils. Several local authorities have done this. One of the most detailed and helpful was produced in Birmingham in collaboration with Birmingham Central Mosque. In 2002 Education Bradford issued detailed and helpful guidelines for schools about Ramadan and this was nationally available on the website of the Muslim Council of Britain. There is still a great and urgent need for central government to provide guidance.

In accordance with a recommendation in the Stephen Lawrence Inquiry report, every local authority is now required to collect information from its schools about racist incidents. There is no national guidance, however, on how the reports are to be compiled and used. Similarly, there is no guidance on how racism is to be defined. Many local authorities have issued useful guidance themselves. But unfortunately, they

---

Box 27

Colour, background, culture or religion
– a definition of racism written by school pupils

Racism is something someone does or says that offends someone else in connection with their colour, background, culture or religion.

Racism is:

- when a person is teased or called names because of their culture or the colour of their skin, their religion, the country they come from, their language and the way they talk, the food they eat, clothes they wear or their background

- when people are stereotyped by their colour or religion

- when a person is rejected or excluded from a group because of their colour or religion

- when people make fun of a person's family

- when a person is treated unfairly because of their way of life.

Source: Preventing and Addressing Racism in Schools, Ealing Education Authority, 2003

---

do not always stress that Islamophobia is a form of racism. This means that incidents of Islamophobia in schools are sometimes not addressed.

Ealing Education Authority, amongst others, has issued extensive documentation about dealing with racism in schools that does include high-profile references to religious hostility. The documentation requires schools to record and report incidents of religious hostility and includes a wide-ranging definition of racism compiled by pupils and students on the regional schools council. It is shown in Box 27. Together with the handbook in which it is embedded,[7] it has been valuable in ensuring that headteachers, governors, staff and education officers are aware of Islamophobia as a matter of professional concern. In addition, and equally importantly, it has raised awareness and commitment amongst pupils and students.

When schools are developing policies and shared views amongst staff and pupils on how to deal with incidents of racism and religious hostility, it is often valuable to discuss real or imaginary situations. Box 28, based on real events from around the country during the war in Iraq in 2003, gives several examples.

The stories in Box 28 also raise questions of professional ethics and of how teachers should deal with matters on which wider society is divided.

Teachers' unions gave valuable guidance and leadership to their members following 11 September

Box 28

We killed hundreds of your lot yesterday
Events and remarks in schools

A bit of teasing
I'm the only Asian teacher at my school. During the war in Iraq a pupil who's also Asian told me that she was being teased by other pupils. 'We killed hundreds of your lot yesterday ... Saddam's your dad, innit ... we're getting our revenge for what you Pakis did to us on 11 September...' I asked her if she had told her class teacher. Yes, she had told her teacher, and her teacher had said: 'Never mind, it's not serious. It'll soon pass. You'll have to expect a bit of teasing at a time like this.'

Not fair
A Year 9 pupil was complaining to me bitterly earlier today. 'All right, I'm overweight and I'm not proud of it. But it really gets to me when other kids go on about it. Last week I lost it. I was out of order, right, but when these two kids said I was fatter than a Teletubby and twice as stupid I swore at them and used the word Paki. I got done for racism and was excluded for a day and my parents were informed and all, and I'm really pissed off, and nothing at all has happened to the kids who wound me up. It's not fair.'

Back door
As a secondary school governor I proposed, following discussions with pupils and parents, that there should be some Islamic Awareness classes at the school on a voluntary basis. 'We'd just be letting Al Qaida in by the back door,' said the chair. The other governors all seemed to agree, or anyway not to bother.

They don't really understand
I'm the parent of children aged 4 and 6. They have been desperately distressed by TV footage from Iraq. I spoke to their class teachers. Both said much the same: 'Yes, a lot of the children seem quite upset. But they'll soon get over it. They don't really understand, you know. Don't worry.'

Crying his eyes out
We're an all-white primary school in rural England. The other day during morning break a boy came running into my office, crying his eyes out. 'The Pakis are coming, the Pakis are coming' he sobbed. I sat him down and calmed him and got him to explain. Apparently, two aeroplanes had flown low over the playground and he had believed they were piloted by terrorists on their way to attack the school.

Just short of treason
In my capacity as deputy head I photocopied an article in the current issue of the journal *Race Equality Teaching* on talking and teaching about the war. I gave a copy to all staff and to a number of governors. One governor, who is also a local councillor, has written to me today: 'I regard the document as highly offensive, politically and racially inflammatory and only just short of treason ... This country is at war with Iraq whether we like it or not; the decision to go to war was made by the democratically elected government of this country and it is not for a teacher to promote anti-war propaganda in this way. As a matter of urgency I request you to repudiate the document.'

Source: various real events in spring and summer 2003

Box 29

Listening to what they were saying
– stories from two schools

Bushra Nasir, Headteacher of Plashet School in East London, recalls 18 months of teaching amid the background noise of tension and war. 'The period after September 11 was a very difficult time,' she said. 'Some pupils were very frightened and very upset. Others were getting all sorts of pressure. Some girls had brothers who were going around saying 'well done' to the hijackers. They felt pressure from all angles.

'There was some anger. Kids were being bombarded with Sept 11 all the time. Some girls were saying there are people killed in Iraq every day and we don't have a minute's silence.'

As in schools around the country, meetings were held and it was decided that openness was the best policy. It is a policy that has continued throughout the ensuing war in Afghanistan and the invasion of Iraq. 'On the day of the invasion of Afghanistan there was a very sombre atmosphere,' said Mrs Nasir.

'The most important thing we found was to listen to what the children were saying and to try to get the correct information across to them,' said Mrs Nasir. 'Our main aim was to put across the value of life and that anything that destroys that from any angle is unacceptable.'

Abdullah Trevathan, Headteacher of Brondesbury School, a privately-funded Muslim school for boys in north-west London, remembers a difficult time.

'It was pretty traumatic,' he said. 'On the surface you wouldn't necessarily have seen anything different.

'But kids tend to take the blame. In this kind of situation they feel responsible and think it's their fault. They ask, is my community responsible for this? Are my parents responsible? Am I responsible for this?' The school contacted the local authority's educational psychology service to make sure students and teachers were supported.

'There was some erratic behaviour,' he said. 'Emotions were running high. Our policy was to give children space to think and to ensure they knew they could talk about how they were feeling.' Our pupils had some name-calling and some spitting, but we were also inundated with letters of support from around the country.'

With pupils from 15 countries and almost every continent, Mr Trevathan said world events have a direct influence within the classroom and the playground. He said: 'In this school we have Afghani kids, Palestinian kids, Iraqi kids. In general we have to watch the news carefully because what happens in the world does affect us personally.'

Source: interviews by Laura Smith, summer 2003

and during the ensuing wars.[8] In Box 29 there are case studies from two schools showing how they responded to international events in the period 2001/03.

Concluding note

This chapter on education should not be read in separation from the next chapter, on community cohesion. There is much in the next chapter that could as easily be placed here. By the same token, there is much in this chapter that could as easily have been discussed under the heading of community cohesion.

9. STREET AND NEIGHBOURHOOD
Aspects of community cohesion

Summary

This chapter discusses the government's community cohesion agenda. It recalls how the agenda has its roots in northern towns and cities where there are substantial numbers of Muslims. When it was first introduced the agenda was misrepresented and distorted in the media and various conceptual objections to it were dismissed or ignored. It nevertheless has the potential to promote valuable initiatives in local settings.

Unhelpful start

'Ethnic communities scarred by the summer riots,' ran the front page headline of a Sunday newspaper on 9 December 2001, 'should learn English and adopt 'British norms of acceptability'.' The news item below it was an interview with the Home Secretary, David Blunkett.[1] The purpose of the interview and of the news item was to trail four reports on the disturbances of summer 2001 which were to be published two days later.[2] The reports would in their turn set off what would be known as the government's community cohesion agenda. This in its turn had implications for other areas of social policy, including education and training.

The coverage provided by that Sunday's paper was taken up in the rest of the media on the following day. From the point of view of many British Muslims, coverage on those two days was an inauspicious start to a government agenda that in fact had several valuable and creative concerns and that was – and continues to be – extremely relevant to addressing Islamophobia, particularly at local levels.

In addition to the four reports published in December 2001 there was the important report by Lord Ouseley about Bradford published a few months earlier. And in due course significant documents would be published by the Local Government Association, the Inter Faith Network, the Home Office and the Inner Cities Religious Council of the Office of the Deputy Prime Minister. A project known as the Community Cohesion Pathfinder Programme was set up and came into operation from April 2003. Fourteen local authorities or consortia were involved: Bury, Charnwood, East Lancashire, Kirklees, Leicester, Mansfield, Middlesbrough, Peterborough, Plymouth, Rochdale, Sandwell, Southwark, Stoke on Trent and West London.[3]

The community cohesion agenda has a range of components and concerns and these vary between local authorities. There is no question of one size fitting all. This chapter considers the agenda's potential to address and reduce Islamophobia at street, neighbourhood and local levels, and to involve local authorities and the voluntary sector in a range of valuable co-operative activities and programmes. In doing so, it considers one particular aspect of the potential: the opportunity to apply to urban areas in Britain the insights, concepts and practical approaches which have been developed over the last 40 years in the academic field of conflict and peace research. The field has its principal centres of gravity in Norway, Germany, Canada and the United States and there are also important institutes in India, Japan and South Africa. In the United Kingdom, the Department of Peace Studies at the University of Bradford is a significant centre of study and research and, even more relevantly, there is a substantial body of research-based knowledge in Northern Ireland.[4]

This chapter discusses aspects of conflict theory. But first, there is a further brief note about the interview with the Home Secretary which introduced the agenda to the general public. He was asked: 'Have we been too tolerant of enforced marriage?' The complete answer to this question was as follows:

> Enforced marriages and youngsters under the age of 16 being whistled away to the Indian sub-continent, genital mutilation and practices that may be acceptable in parts of Africa, are unacceptable in Britain.
>
> We need to be clear we don't tolerate the intolerable under the guise of cultural difference.
>
> We have norms of acceptability and those who come into our home – for that is what it is – should accept those norms just as we would have to do if we went elsewhere.

In the context of the four reports about to be published, and of the Ouseley report published a few months earlier, the Home Secretary appeared to be saying that Muslim communities in northern cities typically tolerate the intolerable, for example genital mutilation and forced marriages of children under 16, and that that is why some of their younger members had been involved in public disorder earlier in the year. The further implication was that the essential purpose of the community cohesion agenda would be to persuade Muslim communities to mend their ways, so that they become 'acceptable'. For people with long experience of combating racial and religious discrimination, the remarks about 'those who come into our home' were eerily reminiscent of many such remarks over the years by politicians and the media. To cite just one example, they echoed the sentiment in an infamous statement made at the time of the *Satanic Verses* affair in 1989: 'Newcomers are only welcome if they become genuine Britishers and don't stuff their alien cultures down our throats'.[5]

The negative and uninformed generalisations about Muslim communities in northern Britain that introduced the community cohesion agenda were of a piece with the Islamophobia that was rampant in autumn 2001 throughout western societies. They helped give the impression that the reports were principally about 'self-segregation' and 'inward-looking communities' and prevented more measured statements in the Home Secretary's interview being attended to. Further, they provoked widespread suspicion amongst Muslims of the reports themselves.[6] The suspicions were in due course

---

Box 30

The violence of the violated
Lancashire and Yorkshire in 2001

The fires that burned across Lancashire and Yorkshire through the summer of 2001 signalled the rage of young Pakistanis and Bangladeshis of the second and third generations, deprived of futures, hemmed in on all sides by racism, failed by their own leaders and representatives and unwilling to stand by as first fascists and then police officers invaded their streets.

Their violence was ad hoc, improvised and haphazard... The fires ... were lit by the youths of communities falling apart from within, as well as from without; youths whose violence was, therefore, all the more desperate. It was the violence of communities fragmented by colour lines, class lines and police lines. It was the violence of hopelessness. It was the violence of the violated.

The Violence of the Violated by Arun Kundnani, 2001

---

strengthened when it emerged that Muslim members of the Cantle committee felt that they had been marginalised during the committee's deliberations, and had been unable to secure adequate attention to Islamophobia and recognition of Muslim identity.[7] Alternative views of the disturbances were published by, amongst others, the Islamic Human Rights Commission[8] and the Institute of Race Relations. There is an extract from the latter report in Box 30.

The concept of cohesion

The concept of cohesion was central to the arguments on multiculturalism in Britain by the Commission on the Future of Multi-Ethnic Britain, chaired by Lord Parekh.[9] But unlike the government, the commission stressed that cohesion is only one value amongst others. Two other, equally important, social values, it argued, are equality and respect for significant difference. The three core values of cohesion, equality and respect for difference, are like the three legs of a stool; if any one of them is de-emphasised the other two are damaged also. In a lecture on cohesion organised by the Runnymede Trust in autumn 2002, Lord Parekh explained the concept of cohesion as follows:

> A society is cohesive if (a) its members have a common commitment to the well-being of the community and are related to each other in a way that they are not related to outsiders; (b) its members are able to find their way around in it, that is, they know how to navigate their way through their society, if they understand its conceptual and cultural grammar, and know how to relate to each other; and (c) its members share a climate of mutual trust, and know that were they to make sacrifices today for the wider community, it will take care of them when the need arises.

The Future of Multi-Ethnic Britain pointed out also that a cohesive democracy must accept disagreements, differences and disobedience, and it commended and reprinted in this respect the distinctions between closed and open approaches to disagreement proposed by the Commission on British Muslims and Islamophobia (see chapter 4 above). Further, such a democracy must vigorously tackle racism in its various forms, including for example Islamophobia and the kinds of institutional racism in public institutions identified and described by the Stephen Lawrence Inquiry report (see chapter 2). The reports on northern cities and the government's ensuing policy documentation about community cohesion contained little engagement with such views. For this reason, and because they similarly showed no awareness of the arguments set out by the Institute of Race Relations (Box 30), they were an uncertain basis for action or for evaluation. They were, however, accompanied by quite substantial funding programmes. These led to some valuable projects, as outlined later in this chapter. It remains (in early 2004) to be seen whether they lead also to useful development of theory. Two Home Office papers published in 2003 were not promising, at least with regard to addressing Islamophobia and recognising British Muslim identity.

The concept of community

The Future of Multi-Ethnic Britain gave considerable attention to the meaning of the term community. It acknowledged that the term usually refers to

something rather amorphous, but pointed out that nevertheless it can have legal significance, as for example in Northern Ireland. *The Oxford English Dictionary* defines it as 'a body of people having a religion, a profession, etc, in common ... a fellowship of interests ... a body of nations unified by common interests'. This definition reflects the fact that in everyday usage terms such as the following are all fairly familiar: 'the local community', 'a valued member of the community', 'the disabled community', 'a mining community', 'the scientific community', 'the gay and lesbian community', 'the two communities in Northern Ireland'. It would be consistent with the dictionary definition to envisage the United Kingdom as a community whose four principal constituent parts are England, Northern Ireland, Scotland and Wales, and also to envisage each of the constituent parts as a community, as also each separate region, city, town or borough. Any one individual belongs to several different communities. This was vividly illustrated in a statement made to the Bradford Commission in 1996:

> I could view myself as a member of the following communities, depending on the context and in no particular order: Black, Asian, Azad Kashmiri, Mirpuri, Jat, Marilail, Kungriwalay, Pakistani, English, British, Yorkshireman, Bradfordian, from Bradford Moor ... I could use the term 'community' in any of these contexts and it would have meaning. Any attempt to define me only as one of these would be meaningless.

Since communities overlap and interact, and since every individual belongs to more than one community, it is helpful to picture Britain as a community of communities rather than as a single monolithic whole. Similarly each town or city – Bradford, Burnley and Oldham, for example – may appropriately be pictured as a community of communities. A cohesive town or city is made up of cohesive communities in constant interaction with each other. Also, it shows due regard for the rights of individuals, not just for the rights of members of communities. The commission's full phrase to evoke the kind of society it commended was 'a community of communities and citizens'.

In the context of the brief discussions above around the concepts of cohesion and community, there are notes below on theories of conflict and on the

Box 31

The meaning of community
Features and feelings

Being a somebody
A community gives its members a sense of belonging, and therefore of their identity and dignity. Here in my community I am among my own people, I am at home, I know them and understand them, and they know and understand me. We speak the same language (including the same body language!), smile or laugh at the same jokes, know the same stories and music, have shared memories. I am recognised and respected, I feel that I am a somebody, not a nonentity.

Being looked after
The members of a community take an interest in each other and have a sense of responsibility towards each other. They are prepared to pay taxes or subscriptions for the common good, or to help less fortunate members, and to donate their time to maintaining the community, whether formally or informally. I feel that I will be looked after if I fall on bad times, and that – for example – my children or my elderly and sick parents will be looked after if they get lost.

Feeling grateful
The members of a community are grateful to it, in so far as it does indeed give them a sense of belonging, identity and dignity. My gratitude may take the form of great affection and love, even self-sacrifice, but may also be expressed through criticism and questioning. Sometimes gratitude is expressed more by caring criticism than by blind devotion.

Family quarrels
Communities are not marked by cosiness alone. There are often arguments, quarrels, and profound disagreements. Jockeyings for power and prestige, internal politics, alliances, betrayals. Expulsion or secession is frequently an option. But essentially quarrels within a community are family quarrels. I have a commitment to staying. I cherish the community, and am prepared to compromise in order that the community itself may be maintained.

A range of belongings
Boundaries round a community can be quite hard and fast, making it difficult to join or leave voluntarily. But often they are fluid, unfixed. It is in any case entirely possible for someone to be a member – a significant member – of several different communities at the same time; indeed, this is usual. I have, and nearly all people have, a range of belongings, identities and loyalties, and sometimes these are out of tune with each other, or are in blatant conflict.

Symbols
A community is held together by symbols and ceremonies which mean the same to all its members. All the following can have symbolic, not just functional, power, and can help bind a community together symbolically: food; buildings and monuments; rites of passage relating to birth, adolescence, marriage and death; clothes (including of course uniforms and insignia); religious worship; music – particularly, perhaps, singing; various courtesies, customs, manners and rules of procedure; and ritualised conflict in sport and games of all kinds. I belong through symbols.

Source: adapted slightly from The Future of Multi-Ethnic Britain, Profile Books 2000.

approach to reducing conflict known as the contact hypothesis. Both sets of notes draw on lessons from Northern Ireland.

Theories of conflict

The cohesion report by government ministers, known as the Denham report, included the assertion that 'ignorance is an obvious sources [*sic*] of conflict' (paragraph 2.10). The unfortunate typographical error implied hasty drafting and proof-reading. But more serious was the conceptual over-simplification. For it is as true to say that a conflictual situation begets and nourishes ignorance as to say that ignorance is a source of conflict. The emphasis that the Denham report laid on removing ignorance, rather than – for example – on action to tackle the sources of conflict in urban and industrial decline, meant that the community cohesion agenda risked being insufficiently robust.[10] The Ritchie report on Oldham, however, was much more explicit about economic and industrial history and about the context in which community cohesion happens or does not happen. There is an extract from the Ritchie report on this topic in Box 32.

The approach to conflict pioneered by the Norwegian theorist Johan Galtung is built on the customary distinctions between (a) attitudes and assumptions (b) behaviours and (c) conflicts of interest and clashes of goals. If the distinctions are applied to the community cohesion agenda, the focus is on (a) the views of themselves and each other that communities hold (b) events such as the disturbances in summer 2001 and (c) underlying conflicts of interest, themselves rooted in industrial, colonial and economic history. Galtung points out that the notion that A (attitudes and assumptions) leads to B (violent behaviour) leads to C (conflict) is over-simplifying, although attractive to common sense. Instead of a visual model that could be summarised as A → B → C, he proposes a triangle:

The triangle model visualises the argument that the relationships between A, B and C are two-way, with each of them being both cause and consequence of the

---

> ### Look first at industrial history
> #### A brief history of Oldham
>
> *Box 32*
>
> ... We have to look first at the industrial history of the town. In the late 19th century, Oldham produced 30 per cent of the world's spun cotton, and a very large proportion of the machinery used in textile production. Other industries had a foothold in Oldham, and at one time there was significant coal-mining, but their importance compared with cotton spinning was always minor, and there were few towns as wholly dependent on one industry as Oldham.
>
> This had two main consequences relevant to our review. The first was that much of the employment in Oldham was relatively low skilled and, except for a few boom periods, relatively low paid. Despite efforts to improve the employment base of the town as the cotton industry declined Oldham has remained, relatively, a poor town.
>
> ... The second consequence of heavy dependence on a single industry was that, as working conditions and expectations improved in the nation generally, it became harder for mill owners to recruit people for unsocial work such as night shifts which were essential to the economy of their enterprises. So people willing to work these shifts were encouraged to migrate, initially from Pakistan, later from Bangladesh, which laid the foundations for the current Pakistani and Bangladeshi communities within the town. The first group of these migrants began to arrive in the 1960s, men first, followed by their families.
>
> *Source: One Oldham One Future (the Ritchie report), 2001*

other two. It follows that the promotion of community cohesion – or, in conflict theory, the resolution of conflict and the making and maintaining of peace – requires a three-pronged approach: (a) action to change attitudes and assumptions (b) action to reduce violence and (c) action to resolve, or at least manage, conflict. All too often the distinction between violence and conflict is not made, and on the contrary the terms 'violence' and 'conflict' are used interchangeably. ('It is the failure to transform conflict,' writes Galtung, 'that leads to violence.') In consequence it is even more difficult than otherwise to distinguish between different forms of violence, and between different ways of managing and resolving conflict.[11]

The contact hypothesis

It was essentially as a consequence of economic and social history and of discriminatory housing policies, the Ritchie report argued, not as a consequence of the refusal or disinclination of South Asian communities to integrate, as the Home Secretary seemed to maintain, that great gulfs formed from the 1960s onwards between white working class communities in Oldham and the newly formed communities from Pakistan and Bangladesh. The gulfs were poignantly described by Ritchie as follows:

> For many white people the attitude seems to be that we would rather the Asians were not here, we will have as little to do with them as possible, and so we pretend that the Asians are not here.

> For many Asians, the attitude seems to be that this is a difficult and alien environment in which we find ourselves, we must protect ourselves from it and its corrupting influences, and we can do that best by creating largely separated communities in Oldham modelled on what we have left behind in Pakistan and Bangladesh.

> ...One consequence of separate development has been the growth of myths...

The myths identified by Ritchie certainly have to be addressed. But even more importantly, the sources of myths in economic and social history have to be identified. Otherwise, measures intended to dispel myths are likely to backfire, and to do more harm than good. The 'parallel lives' which the Ritchie, Cantle and Ouseley reports all describe are a real issue to be addressed. But to claim that they are the fundamental problem, unrelated to history, racism and Islamophobia, is to misperceive them.

The community cohesion agenda appears at times to have a naïve faith that if only there were more contact between different communities all would be well. The contact hypothesis, as it is known, has been much debated by researchers since it was first proposed in the United States in the 1950s. It is attractive to common sense, and also to any political programme

disinclined to look at economic history, or at class conflict and inequality, or at structural racism and disparities of power.[12] But it is repudiated by dramatic events such the recent conflicts in the Balkans and Ruanda. Twelve per cent of all marriages in Yugoslavia, and forty per cent in Sarajevo, were mixed. But this extensive inter-group contact did not prevent traumatic violence and bloodshed at the time of crisis. In Ruanda, there was extensive contact on a day-to-day basis between Tutsi and Hutu; but here too, contact did not prevent people attacking and massacring their former neighbours.[13]

Such cautionary examples must be kept in mind. But a leading social psychologist who has made many extensive studies of inter-group contact over the years, and who is thoroughly familiar with research in many different countries, summarises the current state of research knowledge with a simple question and answer:

> Does contact work? *Yes*.[14]

Contact works, he showed, by affecting attitudes and assumptions, namely the 'A' point in Galtung's triangle (see above). Contact reduces suspicion, anxiety and sense of threat; there is a corresponding increase in mutual trust; the outgroup is seen as more various than before and more open to change; and there may be a re-examining of history and an inclination to forgive the outgroup for past deeds and atrocities, whether real or imagined. In the terms used in chapter 3 of this report, there can be a move from 'closed' views of other people to 'open' ones. Attitude changes of these kinds can lead to, and be reinforced by, cooperative activities and projects of various kinds, and shared loyalties and commitments, for example a shared commitment to maintaining relationships within and between communities in good repair; shared civic pride; shared stories, imagery and symbols; and shared struggle.

Research with school pupils and students in Northern Ireland has shown that the contact hypothesis is warranted if some or most of the following conditions apply:

- There is 'single identity work' as well. This involves members of a singe community exploring their own identities, hopes and anxieties and relating these to the views they hold of non-members. Such work may be a valuable prelude to contact with the outgroup, or may alternatively accompany and complement such contact. Either way it needs to examine issues of gender identity as well as ethnic, religious and cultural identity, and needs to adopt a holistic approach to adolescent concerns and to peer-group pressures[15]

- Contact is part of a multi-layered approach – there is attention not only to the perceptions, stories, biographies and day-to-day experiences of individuals but also to the wider social processes and narratives in which these are interpreted and perpetuated

- There is equal status between groups when they meet

- Participants are involved in a cooperative venture with common goals, not for example in a win-lose situation such as a sports fixture

- The contact has institutional support

- It is accepted that conflict and misperception are 'inter-generational', namely that they are of long standing and are passed from one generation to another. Short-term interventions are not enough.

Concluding note

The Home Office interim report of autumn 2003 noted that the concept of community cohesion needs to be explained 'in simple, meaningful and direct terms'.[16] It did not, however, envisage that providing such explanations would involve re-visiting the definition that had been proposed in 2001 by the Local Government Association and that has been widely adopted. 'Setting out to create a new definition,' it declared, 'is too time-consuming and confusing for many participants.' It is nevertheless the case that, in the words of an old adage, 'there's nothing so practical as a good theory'. The community cohesion agenda got off to a poor start, for it appeared unambiguously to be based on negative views and stereotypes of British Muslim communities and to be proposing mere assimilation rather than genuine inclusion. Sound theorising is needed if the agenda is to be put on a more promising course.

If the agenda is pursued and enriched by the insights of conflict theory, however, and with due awareness of the limits and value of inter-community contacts, it has potential to make a significant difference. There are valuable insights in this connection from Northern Ireland, particularly if Islamophobia is seen, analysed and addressed as a form of racism that is similar to sectarianism.

A recurring note throughout this report is that Islamophobia has specific characteristics, and that action to combat it must not be left to chance within larger campaigns, policies and programmes. The community cohesion agenda needs to be far more explicit than it has been so far about issues of Islamophobia and British Muslim identity. Such explicitness will make it easier to tackle what the Home Office admits are 'difficult issues' – criminality and drugs amongst some young Muslims, for example, and aspects of leadership and authority within some Muslim communities, and the attractions in some communities of 'westophobia'.

In relation to explicitness about Islamophobia and difficult issues, a crucial role is played by the national and local media. This is the subject of the next chapter.

10. DEALING WITH THE MEDIA
Towards a code of professional ethics

Summary

This chapter cites examples of negative coverage in the media and discusses the respective roles of the Press Complaints Commission, professional ethics amongst journalists, and lobbying by organisations and individuals.

A nice Welsh girl like you

Critics often lambast the media as one homogenous group, but that is a mistake. It has the quirks, divisions and points of departure that one would expect in any diverse community. Even so, the complaints one so often hears about lazy, stereotypical and factually inaccurate coverage of events involving Muslim communities and the Islamic faith often ring true. For example, the story told in Box 33 by Merryl Wyn Davies, a Muslim convert in Wales, sounds all too plausible. Whenever she is interviewed by a journalist, she says, the first question is 'How does a nice, sensible Welsh girl like you end up joining a religion of militant fundamentalists who suppress women?'

Many people (66 per cent according to a 2002 YouGov opinion poll finding) draw most if not all of their information about Islam and the Muslim communities from the media. The media have a distinctive responsibility, therefore, to present 'open' views of Islam as distinct from 'closed' (as outlined in chapter 4). This point was made graphically by comedian Shazia Mirza in an interview conducted for this report. There are relevant extracts in Box 34.

After 9/11 there was genuine recognition among most media outlets of the need to avoid material that would inflame the relationship between Muslims and non-Muslims in Britain. Led by the line from Downing Street, even the *Sun* – long saddled with a reputation as a racially intolerant and sensationalist newspaper – issued a high profile appeal for calm. On September 13, 2001, a full-page article written by David Yelland – then the editor – proclaimed *Islam is Not an Evil Religion*. It may have been stating the obvious. But at the time it made a valuable contribution – a fact recognised by the Commission for Racial Equality

---

Box 33

The world I inhabit
Stereotypes in the media

How does a nice, sensible Welsh girl like you end up joining a religion of militant fundamentalists who suppress women?'

Interviewers have endlessly asked me this question. The question is predicated on the proposition that nice and sensible people do not become Muslims, and by implication therefore that no Muslim is either nice or sensible.

The lack of niceness or reason is proved by the second assertion: Muslims in totality, and presumably by their nature, are militant. Militancy is synonymous with the dread word fundamentalist that clearly needs no definition. The logical consequence of militant fundamentalism is the self-evident observation that all Muslims suppress women. In the perception of the interviewer these terms belong together, because Islam offers no alternative. Become a Muslim and that is what you get.

Of course, interviewers often play devil's advocate, asking aggressive questions to stimulate robust rebuttal. In which case, they must be aware of the possibility of an alternative view. So why does it never occur to them that devilishly reductive stereotypes actually impede and often preclude sensible discussion of the alternative view?

Neither the conventional questions nor the rote answers they are designed to elicit describe or help anyone understand who I am, the world I inhabit, how I know and understand Islam, and the condition of being a Muslim.

Box 34

Twice as funny as white males
Interview with Shazia Mirza

... It's okay to laugh at what I am saying. Initially it wasn't. Especially after September 11, people were scared to laugh. They'd never seen a Muslim woman in the entertainment business. Stand-up was really white male dominated. It was like, 'Oh my God, there's a Muslim woman on the stage. We really can't listen to what she is saying, we must respect her.'

When I wear my hijab on stage, I have to prove myself. People have so many perceptions of you before you even open your mouth. I have to be twice as funny as white male comedians. They perceive women not to be funny and Muslim women never to have left the house. I really have to prove myself twice over. But once people warm to me and they realise my hijab is nothing to do with me, they forget about it. They almost don't notice it's there.

Now that I am better known I can talk about suicide bombers and people laugh, but if I'd done that three years ago it would have been impossible. I do jokes about them to defuse their importance and to say they don't represent all of us and that we wouldn't blow ourselves and others up even if someone forced us to do it.

... I think perceptions of Muslims have got worse. First there was September 11. Now there is Abu Hamza, Finsbury Park mosque, and his pronouncements about producing young fanatics. From what people see on television, they must believe that we are all terrorists, that Muslim women are really oppressed and they are beaten up by their husbands and that the men all have beards and teach their sons to be suicide bombers. The West must think we have no values for life and we are all crazy.

It's very difficult to look to the future because people are never going to give up their religion. You can't tell someone to stop being so religious because those are that person's beliefs. If things are to change there has to be a greater understanding of our faith and it has to be the truth. At the moment the case isn't being told. People see the extreme version of Muslims on television, programmes like that episode of Spooks showing the recruitment of suicide bombers. I'm sure it does go on but it's not a good image to give the public. That kind of stereotyping alienates both sides. The average white person will look at that and think that's what we're all like. And young Muslim kids will feel attacked by the West and Britain and their reaction is one of anger. They start to believe that the police and politicians don't understand them.

which shortlisted the article for a Race In The Media Award.

Representation

As the shock from September 11 subsided, however, Muslim concern about the media's tendency to elevate fringe figures to a place of mainstream importance became a live issue once again.[1] For many years Muslims had complained about the prominence given to Omar Bakri Muhammed – the North London cleric with a penchant for publicity and the provocative quote. For all the good intentions, after September 11 many newspapers and broadcasters still found him a hard habit to break. But the appeal of Omar Bakri

paled dramatically when set against the attractions of Abu Hamza. Here, just waiting for an unquestioning press, was a villain straight out of central casting. He has an eye patch, a hook replacing an amputated hand, a claimed association with Taliban training camps and a knack for issuing blood-curdling threats.

In an analysis of the media post September 11, the *Daily Mail* printed the same photo of Abu Hamza on the 15th, 17th, 18th, 20th and 21st.[2] It also printed an interview with him on the 13th September that was partially repeated on the 15th and 18th as well. Days after the beginning of the war in Iraq, his views were sought again. The Press Association, which supplies all national and regional papers, described him as 'one of Britain's best known Muslim preachers'. For journalists from the *Telegraph* to the Today Programme, and from the *News of The World* to Newsnight, he was a top attraction.

Of course, figures like Hamza and his associates have a right to have their views reported, as does any other citizen of this country. But too often such views are reported as representative of all Muslim communities. Moderates who sought to place them in their proper context struggled to make their voices heard. Inayat Bunglawala of the Muslim Council of Britain voiced the frustrations of many. 'There are over 800 mosques in the UK and only one of them is run by a known radical. Yet this one mosque (Finsbury Park, London) seems to get more coverage than all the rest put together! The situation is akin to taking a member of the racist BNP and saying his views are representative of ordinary Britons.'[3]

Ahmed Versi, the editor of the *Muslim News,* says that frustration remains. 'The Muslim community is attacked for not denouncing September 11 enough, yet the newspapers and television news will give an enormous amount of space and airtime to people like Abu Hamza and not seek out moderate voices. He is a nothing figure in the Muslim community. He doesn't have a major following. Young Muslim men are not particularly attracted to his teachings. So why do newspapers continue to give him so much space? It is Islamophobia.'

A safe haven

The British media is grappling with three truths. The Government is concerned about the number of asylum seekers coming to Britain. It also faces a very real threat from terrorism. Some of the potential terrorists are Muslim. It is when these phenomena merge that some of the most divisive reporting occurs. The most obvious example was the tragic murder of Detective Constable Stephen Oake, who was killed during an anti-terrorist raid in Manchester. The suspect, it later transpired, was an Algerian asylum seeker. Consequently the story had the two ingredients necessary for a post-9/11 law and order scandal. The fact that several of the Algerians arrested a few weeks earlier for allegedly producing the deadly toxin ricin in a north London apartment had applied for asylum added spice to an already heady brew.

Box 35

Essentially foreign
Some findings from research

A study was made of all articles on British Muslims that appeared in *The Guardian/Observer* and *The Times/Sunday Times* in the period 1993-97. There were 837 articles altogether, 504 in the *Guardian/Observer* and 333 in *The Times/Sunday Times*. In addition stories about British Muslims in 1997 were studied in the *Sun* and the *Mail*. A count was also made of stories about Muslims in the wider world. The findings of the research included:

Only one story in seven was about Islam in Britain, as distinct from the wider world. The implication was that Islam is essentially foreign.

Muslims in Britain were frequently represented as irrational and antiquated, threatening British liberal values and democracy.

The agenda of Muslims in Britain was seen as being dictated by Muslims outside Britain.

A strong focus on extremist and fanatical Muslims marginalised the moderate and pragmatic stance of the majority of British Muslims.

Muslims in Britain were depicted as being involved in deviant activities, for example corruption and crime.

The *Guardian* gave much more coverage to Muslim issues than other papers and was more likely to write positively and to provide alternative viewpoints. It is read by far fewer people than most other papers, however, and its secular, human rights stance means Islam is sometimes formulated as offensive to its liberal norms.

Commenting later on the findings, the author noted that Muslims are becoming a more powerful lobbying force and have made efforts to create a representative body, the Muslim Council of Britain, with which the government can negotiate. She judged that lobbying by Muslims has had a positive effect on both the government and the media.

Source: the research was undertaken by Dr Elizabeth Poole, University of Staffordshire. It is published in Reporting Islam, I.B.Tauris, 2002.

While the link between terrorism, asylum and the Muslim faith makes for the most inflammatory stories, the formula can work with just two of the three ingredients. In the case of Abdul Salam, there was no suggestion that he was a terrorist, but he was wanted for a grisly murder in Brussels. The *Sun's* version of the story, published in January 2003 began 'A stalker wanted over the murder of a woman in Belgium is an asylum-seeker hiding in Britain.' Later in the text, readers were told: 'Devout Muslim Salam vanished a few hours before British cops were about to swoop on him over the killing.' Given that the crime did not appear to have any particular religious connotations or motivation, would a similar report concerning another suspect have used the description 'Devout Catholic Fred Smith'?

Whose watchdog?

In July 2001, a month before the US terrorist atrocities, senior officials from the Muslim press and the Muslim Council of Britain met with Lord Wakeham, then the chairman of the Press Complaints Commission. Together the learned gathering discussed the 'negative stereotyping' of Muslims and Lord Wakeham assured those present that he understood their concerns. On November 15, amid the pleas for calm and mutual tolerance and the establishment of Islam Awareness Week to promote greater understanding across the communities, the *Daily Express* published an article by columnist Carol Sarler which seemed to encapsulate all of the worries conveyed to Lord Wakeham just four months previously.

Under the headline *Why do I have to Tolerate the Rantings of Bigots just because they are Muslim*, Ms Sarler said even she, as a 'conscientious, secular liberal' felt unable to voice legitimate doubts about the Islamic faith and its adherents. The irony of the fact that she was doing so over an entire page of a national newspaper did not trouble her. Citing one single opinion poll which, she said, showed 70 per cent of British Muslims either support or condone Osama bin Laden, she said: 'We are constantly told that the vast majority of Moslems in this country are moderates and hush your mouth if you even might think, oh really, so where are they then?' She said many refer to Islam as 'a religion of tolerance, peace and love', adding: 'Which is jolly splendid but goes nowhere

towards explaining why every Moslem state in the world today is a cauldron of violence, corruption, oppression and dodgy democracy: the direct opponents of everything a liberal holds dear; yet at your peril do you mention it.' The Qur'an she dismissed as 'no more than a bloodthirsty little book'. If her target had been Christianity, the equivalent insult would have been 'Jesus was no more than a bloodthirsty little man'.

On the day of publication, an *Express* reader submitted a complaint to the Press Complaints Commission, still led by Lord Wakeham, on the grounds that the article was discriminatory and inaccurate. But the complaint was rejected. In its adjudication, the PCC accepted the *Express's* argument that 'the article, headed as comment, was clearly distinguished as the opinion of the columnist, in accordance with terms of the Code'. It noted the *Express* printed an article of rebuttal from the Muslim Council of Britain (MCB) the following week. Other complaints from the MCB have been rejected on the grounds that individuals have a right to reply if inaccurate reports are printed about them, but not organisations on behalf of a religious faith.[4] The PCC said: 'Clause 13 (Discrimination) relates only to named individuals and, as in the article no specific persons were subject to prejudiced or pejorative attack based upon their race or religion, did not consider that a breach of that clause could be established.' There are no plans to close this loophole, even when the new press regulator assumes responsibility.

What also disturbed many was the fact that the PCC seems unable or unwilling to act even when many of the comments made by the author are based on claims that are themselves open to challenge. For example, the columnist claimed that few Muslim leaders had spoken out against 9/11. In point of fact the MCB issued a condemnatory press release within three hours of the atrocity on 11 September and within 48 hours convened a meeting of community leaders, from which emerged a joint statement denouncing the atrocities as 'indefensible'.[5]

It is clear that the PCC is not an adequate bulwark against Islamophobia in the media. A more reliable bulwark, if it can be created, would lie in a revised code of professional ethics. An example of a code published in the United States is given in Box 36.[6]

Box 36

Representing Muslims and Arabs
Guidelines for journalists

Visual images

Seek out people from a variety of ethnic and religious backgrounds when photographing Americans mourning those lost in New York, Washington and Pennsylvania.

Seek out people from a variety of ethnic and religious backgrounds when photographing rescue and other public service workers and military personnel.

Do not represent Arab Americans and Muslims as monolithic groups. Avoid conveying the impression that all Arab Americans and Muslims wear traditional clothing.

Use photos and features to demystify veils, turbans and other cultural articles and customs.

Stories

Seek out and include Arabs and Arab Americans, Muslims, South Asians and men and women of Middle Eastern descent in all stories about the war, not just those about Arab and Muslim communities or racial profiling.

Cover the victims of harassment, murder and other hate crimes as thoroughly as you cover the victims of overt terrorist attacks.

Make an extra effort to include olive-complexioned and darker men and women, Sikhs, Muslims and devout religious people of all types in arts, business, society columns and all other news and feature coverage, not just stories about the crisis.

Seek out experts on military strategies, public safety, diplomacy, economics and other pertinent topics who run the spectrum of race, class, gender and geography.

When writing about terrorism, remember to include white supremacist, radical anti-abortionists and other groups with a history of such activity.

Do not imply that kneeling on the floor praying, listening to Arabic music or reciting from the Qur'an are peculiar activities.

When describing Islam, keep in mind there are large populations of Muslims around the world, including in Africa, Asia, Canada, Europe, India and the United States.

Distinguish between various Muslim states; do not lump them together as in constructions such as 'the fury of the Muslim world.'

Avoid using word combinations such as 'Islamic terrorist' or 'Muslim extremist' that are misleading because they link whole religions to criminal activity. Be specific: alternate choices, depending on context, include 'Al Qaeda terrorists' or, to describe the broad range of groups involved in Islamic politics, 'political Islamists.'

Do not use religious characterizations as shorthand when geographic, political, socio-economic or other distinctions might be more accurate.

Avoid using terms such as 'jihad' unless you are certain of their precise meaning and include the context when they are used in quotations. The basic meaning of 'jihad' is to exert oneself for the good of Islam and to better oneself.

Consult the Library of Congress guide for transliteration of Arabic names and Muslim or Arab words to the Roman alphabet. Use spellings preferred by the American Muslim Council, including 'Muhammad,' 'Quran,' and 'Makkah ,' not 'Mecca.'

Regularly seek out a variety of perspectives for your opinion pieces. Check your coverage against the five Maynard Institute for Journalism Education fault lines of race and ethnicity, class, geography, gender and generation.

Ask men and women from within targeted communities to review your coverage and make suggestions.

Source: Association of Professional Journalists, Indianapolis, 2002.

The internet

The world wide web and internet chatrooms have brought new difficulties for those trying to urge moderation on the mass media. Few procedures exist to regulate content on the web. Every citizen can be a pundit. Whereas more established media are subject to the laws of libel and the incitement provisions of the various pieces of race legislation, virtual anarchy reigns in cyberspace. Even highly regarded, high profile and well intentioned organisations have a difficult time regulating content to ensure they remain inside the law.

The issue has sparked a battle – one of many – between Ken Livingstone, Mayor of London and the London *Evening Standard*. Since October 2002, Mr Livingstone has referred the newspaper to the PCC, the Commission for Racial Equality and the Metropolitan Police for allowing Islamophobic and racist material to appear on its website *This is London*. In October 2002 he complained to the CRE after finding a string of racist messages on the site in the days following the Bali bomb. The postings which formed part of his complaint included the statements: 'Hands up who would like to see, or would agree with, the rounding up of Muslims?', 'Who'd want to live next door to Muslims now?' and 'I'm sorry, but I just don't want any more Muslims in my country; Vote them out of your country. Don't do business with them.' Mr Livingstone said the second complaint, submitted in March, was made after the newspaper broke assurances to him that it would exercise greater control over the website. Comments noted on the second occasion remained on the site for at least a day and a half. They included the thoughts of one chat room user who said: '...Every mosque a potential terrorist HQ.'

The same set of issues will arise on smaller sites, many of which have fewer concerns about their public image and therefore fewer reasons to police themselves or prevent the propagation of stereotypes. In April, on *My Docklands*, a community website in Tower Hamlets – home to Britain's largest Bangladeshi population – the talk was of Muslims and their alleged failings. Referring to his local mosques, one correspondent said: 'These institutions have become a hot bed of hatred wherein young impressionable youths are being brainwashed into fanatical Islamic beliefs which – if you search the internet and look at Islamic sites – you can see that they preach death against all Kafirs (that's you and me!). I've learnt to live in a community that respects everyone and protects them. That is not how you could describe Tower Hamlets.' There is a world of tolerance and enlightenment on the internet. But there's a great deal of unchecked bigotry too.

Dealing with this particular problem is far from straightforward. *This is London* maintains it has a strict editorial policy of removing racially intolerant comments. Officials have expressed disappointment that the mayor did not initially approach the paper's internet division before going public and say action has been taken to improve the monitoring of postings on the website. Such action is welcome because in the absence of co-operation, it is hard to see what effective sanctions can be brought against the owners of websites which carry offensive or Islamophobic material. The PCC regards this as an issue for the CRE, while the CRE points out that it has little or no power under its remit to deal with instances of religious discrimination. The High Court judgement outlined in Box 15, however, may well mean that in future prosecutions can be brought under the Public Order Act.

What can be done?

In a lecture in summer 2002, Brian Whitaker (Middle East editor of *The Guardian* and manager of a website for better understanding of the Arab world) outlined a series of practical suggestions for improving media coverage of Islam.[7] The guidance in Box 37 draws extensively on his proposals. It draws also on points raised earlier in this chapter.

There is a perception in Muslim communities that Islamophobia in the British media is fuelled by supporters of the current government of Israel. Conversely, there is a perception in Jewish communities that antisemitism is spread in part by supporters of the Palestinian cause. Joint projects to address the issues have been organised by the Uniting Britain Trust and in February 2004 a delegation from the Muslim Council of Britain met with the Board of Deputies of British Jews to discuss areas of cooperation between Muslim and Jewish communities. Areas discussed included joint working against xenophobia in order to protect the religious rights of all faith communities in the UK.[8]

Box 37

What can be done?
Ways of improving media coverage

Complaining

- Stereotypes are self-perpetuating unless people challenge them. Once they are challenged, writers tend to back off, or at the least start to qualify them a bit.

- Demand correction of factual errors. If complaining about the use of words, be prepared to suggest alternative terminology.

- Don't try to censor opinions, but engage in debate, for example through letters to the editor or directly to the writers concerned. Some editors and writers will respond positively, though with others it's an apparent waste of time, particularly in the short term.

- If you don't get satisfaction write to the Press Complaints Commission, making sure that your letter is formulated in accordance with the PCC's code of practice. You may not get satisfaction in the short term but persevere, for editors and writers do not like being reported to the PCC and constant complaints may cause them to moderate their views.

- Send copies of your complaint to friends and contacts. Instead or as well, post them on a website. In this way you help to build up a climate of opinion and help persuade others to complain as well.

- Bear in mind that effective complaining requires organisation, both to monitor what is published and to ensure that complaints are formulated in the best possible way.

Employment

- Newspapers and other media should take positive action measures, including bursary schemes for journalists in training, to ensure the recruitment of more employees from Muslim backgrounds. It is important that such people should be part of the mainstream, not ghettoised into writing only or mainly about Muslim issues.

- Throughout the media and other cultural industries key roles are played by 'gatekeepers' – commissioning editors, producers, curators, senior administrators. It is essential that they should be challenged to use their great influence to ensure greater use of writers and performers of Muslim backgrounds.

Education

- There are several excellent websites providing reliable information about Islam and British Muslims. They should be widely publicised amongst all journalists.

- Issues of Islamophobia and British Muslim identity should be on the syllabus of professional training and part of induction programmes.

Professional ethics

- Individual newspapers should draw up codes of practice about how they will cover and report Islam, and should publish these on their websites.

Source: adapted slightly from a lecture by Brian Whitaker, summer 2002.

11. GETTING THERE?
A review of progress, 1997-2004

Summary

This chapter lists the 60 recommendations that were made in the 1997 report of the Commission on British Muslims and Islamophobia, and reviews the progress that has, and has not yet, been made. Undoubtedly there have been improvements. These have been accompanied, however, by increased levels of anti-Muslim prejudice in some quarters and there is still much to do. The chapter closes with a summary of immediate and mid-term priorities for further action.

Government departments, bodies and agencies

All

1) Review equal opportunities policies in employment, service delivery and public consultation, and ensure that these refer explicitly to religion as well as to ethnicity, race and culture

See chapter 7. For several years most government departments have referred to religion in their policy documentation and since December 2003 discrimination on grounds of religion in employment matters has been unlawful, thanks to the EU Employment Directive. There is still no legal requirement, however, to avoid discrimination on religious grounds in service delivery issues. The Commission for Racial Equality did not mention religion in guidance it issued regarding the implementation of the Race Relations (Amendment) Act in 2002.

Education

2) Collect, collate and publish data on the ethnic origins and attainment of pupils in all schools, including independent and grant-maintained schools as well as locally maintained schools

See chapter 8. The Pupil Level Annual Schools' Census (PLASC), operational since January 2002, now allows for pupil level data on the national pupil database to be linked with information about ethnicity and gender.

3) Collect, collate and publish data on the religious affiliations of pupils in all schools

The DfES still does not collect national data on the religious affiliation of pupils. Many individual schools collect this data, however, and so do some local authorities.

4) Review and if necessary modify the criteria and procedures for providing state funding to religiously-based schools, to ensure that they do not discriminate unfairly against Muslim bodies

See chapter 8. There are now (January 2004) four state funded schools. The DfES insists there is a level playing field. Criteria for bidding for capital funding for new schools are published and it says all bids are assessed against the same criteria irrespective of whether they are for faith schools – of whatever faith – or non-faith schools. Since September 1999 decisions on proposals to open a maintained faith school rest with the local school organisation committee (SOC).

5) Make the criteria and procedures for providing state funding to religiously-based schools more transparent, and permit appeals against decisions of the Secretary of State

The Education Act 2002 introduced a new requirement on LEAs where there is a need to set up an additional school. From June 2003, where a local education authority (LEA) decides that an additional, wholly new secondary school is needed, it has to publish a notice inviting other interested parties to bring forward proposals for the school before publishing any proposal of its own. The LEA then has to publish a summary of all the proposals, to enable all local interested parties to comment on the options. The Secretary of State has the final say.

6) Ensure Muslim educationalists, as also educationalists from other faith communities, are involved in discussions of education for citizenship

The Qualifications and Curriculum Authority (QCA) received information and views from organisations and associations from a range of communities and the citizenship education working party held a one day seminar on ethnic diversity and citizenship education. The results were fed in to the QCA's schemes of work for citizenship which were sent to every school. There is no reference to British Muslim identity or to Islamophobia in the schemes of work, notwithstanding the valuable resources that have been published by the Islamic Society of Britain in connection with Islamic Awareness Week and by the Development Education Centre in Birmingham.

7) Conduct a review of good practice in the use of Section 11 funding for English language teaching in schools, and be prepared to permit or encourage greater flexibility in the conditions attached to this funding

This grant, now part of the DfES Standards Fund, has been renamed the Ethnic Minority Achievement Grant (EMAG). It is a ring-fenced grant for activities directly related to raising the attainment of ethnic minority pupils and meeting the particular needs of those pupils for whom English is an additional language (EAL). It was increased in 2003. Several valuable reviews of EAL teaching have been published by Ofsted during the last few years. There is no reference in them to issues of British Muslim identity.

8) Issue formally a set of principles for teaching about religion and citizenship in a multi-faith and multi-ethnic society

See chapter 8. The introduction of citizenship as a statutory subject from September 2002 ensures that for the first time all pupils will be taught about 'the diversity of national, regional, religious and ethnic identities in the UK and the need for mutual respect and understanding'. For example, in the schemes of work developed by QCA there is a unit entitled 'Britain – a Diverse Society'. There is not yet a statement of principles.

9) Develop similar principles about the teaching of history, for example with regard to what pupils learn about the Crusades, and about the spread of Islam over the centuries

The national curriculum includes a statutory requirement for pupils to be taught about the social, cultural, religious and ethnic diversity of the societies studied, both in Britain and the wider world.

Islamic History 700-1250 is an optional study at Key Stage 3 (ages 11-14). There is no statement of principles. In autumn 2003 the DfES set up a mapping project that would list resources currently available for teaching about Islam and issues of Muslim identity throughout all subjects in the national curriculum and it is likely that this will lead to consideration and discussion of overarching principles.

10) Give guidance to registered inspectors on points to look for when reporting on the arrangements schools make for the pastoral, cultural and religious needs of Muslim pupils

A revised framework for school inspections includes an enhanced focus on inclusion and since September 2001 Ofsted has required all school inspectors to have undertaken training on issues relating to ethnic minority pupils. There is no focus in the training on issues of British Muslim identity or Islamophobia.

11) Encourage more Muslims to train as teachers, including for but not only for the teaching of religious education

Ministers say they are keen to recruit more Muslims but the focus of their recruitment drive is ethnicity not religion. The proportion of ethnic minority students enrolling on courses of initial teacher training in England rose from 6 per cent in 1999/00 to 7.8 per cent in 2002/03. At the same time, the total number of entrants rose by 20 per cent. Targets have been agreed with the Teacher Training Agency (TTA) to increase the proportion to nine per cent by 2005/06. It would be possible for these targets to be met without there being any increase in the number of Muslim teachers.

Employment

12) Issue guidelines on good employment practice on matters affecting Muslim employees

See chapter 7. The European Directive on Employment makes religious discrimination illegal in the workplace as of December 2003. Sound guidance by ACAS was published in autumn 2003 and additional guidance was issued by the Muslim Council of Britain and the British Muslim Research Centre in 2004. The latter is available in a range of community languages as well as English.

Health

13) Develop guidelines on good practice in health care relating to religious and cultural needs, including topics such as the following: employment and use of non-Christian chaplains; religious observance; diet and food; respect for cultural and religious norms and injunctions relating to modesty, for example to do with mixed-sex wards and the examination of female patients by male doctors; consultation and contacts with local faith communities; advocacy and befriending services; and general pastoral care in multi-faith settings

The Department of Health reports that it has undertaken a number of consultations with faith communities. 'We have funded the Central Mosque at Regents Park to undertake health fairs and smoking cessation clinics. We are currently planning a workshop with the faith communities to develop an ongoing method of consultation on race and health issues. Many more Muslim chaplains have been employed. There has also been wide consultation on subjects such as the special needs of Muslim burials.' Two reports on spiritual needs were published in autumn 2003 by the Department of Heath and South Yorkshire Workforce Development Confederation but both concentrated more on chaplaincy as a career than on the specific needs of particular faith communities.

Law

14) Make discrimination on religious grounds unlawful

See chapter 7. This has happened on employment issues, though through legal change at European level rather than as a result of a principled commitment from the UK government. Discrimination on religious grounds in service delivery is still permitted. The government's continuing failure to deal robustly with this matter remains a matter of great concern.

15) Ensure that proposed new legislation on racial violence makes reference to religion

See chapter 6. This recommendation was rejected

when the Crime and Disorder Act 1997 came on to the statute book but subsequently the government changed its mind. The law now recognises acts which are 'racially or religiously aggravated' and requires courts to sentence accordingly.

16) When sentencing offenders for crimes of violence or harassment, treat evidence of religious hatred as an aggravating factor, as already with racial violence

See above. This does now happen.

17) Amend the Public Order Act 1986 to make incitement to religious hatred unlawful

See chapter 6. There was consideration of this matter in autumn 2001. The government proposed the amendment but it was rejected by the House of Lords. Subsequently (see Box 15), case law established that the principal harm covered by the concept of incitement to religious hatred (namely, abusive and offensive behaviour) does now attract higher sentences.

18) Review legislation on blasphemy, and include in this a study of relevant legislation in other countries

A House of Lords committee chaired by Viscount Colville in 2002/2003 considered reforming or scrapping the blasphemy laws and introducing legislation outlawing incitement to religious hatred. It was unable to reach consensus.

Monitoring and statistics

19) Give a clear lead on ethnic monitoring, aimed at developing coherence in policy, collection, analysis and use, and spreading the best practice which already exists at many local levels

Monitoring by ethnicity is now much more widespread than in 1997, not least as a result of the Race Relations (Amendment) Act. The DfES has issued helpful guidance on the purposes of monitoring by ethnicity. After much lobbying, a question on religion was inserted at the eleventh hour into the 2001 census and it is likely that substantial cross-tabulations will in due course be published.

20) Give a clear lead on the monitoring of racial and religious violence, such that there is greater comparability between the records of different police districts and monitoring groups

Patchy progress. Neither the Home Office nor the Metropolitan Police yet has reliable figures on violence involving religious hostility.

21) Ensure that there is a question about religion in the 2001 census

See chapter 5. A voluntary question was inserted. Ninety-three per cent of the respondents answered it.

22) Ensure that the 2001 census of population contains a question which enables reliable estimates to be made of the size and demographic features not only of Bangladeshi-background and Pakistani-background communities (as in 1991) but also – amongst others – of Bosnian, Middle Eastern, North African, Somali and Turkish communities

The census asked only for religious affiliation and country of birth. Officials thought further questions would make the exercise too complicated and might reduce the number of responses. The country of birth statistics provide useful estimates of the size of some of the smaller Muslim communities.

23) Provide a breakdown of the broad category 'ethnic minority' in Civil Service monitoring reports and reports on the composition of public bodies, and conduct internal reviews to check whether the South Asian members of the Civil Service and of public bodies appear to include an equitable proportion of Muslims

This is not yet being done.

24) Continue to monitor the composition of the prison population according to the religious affiliations of offenders

Monitoring of the prison population by religious affiliation continues. There has been a significant rise in the numbers of Muslim prisoners. This may be partly due to a rise in the numbers of prisoners who are foreign nationals.

25) Monitor and evaluate immigration and asylum policy according to religion as well as to race and nationality

This is not done. It is clear, however, that a high proportion of refugees and people seeking asylum, perhaps as high as 80 per cent, are from Muslim countries.

The Prime Minister's Office

26) Propose the appointment of Muslims to the House of Lords

Four Muslim peers, Baroness Uddin, Lord Patel, Lord Ahmed and Lord Bhatia now sit in the House of Lords.

Social exclusion

27) Scrutinise measures and programmes aimed at reducing poverty and inequality, for example through the Social Exclusion Unit (SEU) and the Single Regeneration Budget, with regard to their impact on Muslim communities

The SEU and related programmes adopted culture-blind approaches at first (see chapter 6 of the report of the Commission on Multi-Ethnic Britain, 2000). Subsequently the programmes became more sensitive. Muslim groups and organisations are increasingly involved in discussions at local levels and the Muslim Council of Britain has a regeneration committee which has dialogue with government nationally.

The Inner Cities Religious Council, set up in the Department of the Environment in 1992 by the Conservative government, has been sustained and developed by the Labour administrations. The growing Faith Community Unit in the Home Office (from three part time officials in 1999 to fourteen by autumn 2003) is increasingly significant, as are government funding for the Inter-Faith Network, the Employment Forum and Faith Regen UK (a Muslim-led inter-faith regeneration company) and a wide range of national and local faith-based initiatives.

The government's community cohesion agenda (see chapter 9) has potential to increase recognition of Muslim communities in neighbourhood renewal. A valuable guide has been published by NACRO on the involvement of faith communities in community safety issues (McManus 2001).

28) Ensure that measures and programmes aimed at reducing poverty and inequality involve Muslims, as appropriate, at the early planning stages

See note 27 above.

Local and regional statutory bodies

(Please note: information about actions at local and regional levels is by definition not available nationally. The notes that follow are accordingly rather general. Some indicate that it would be valuable if the relevant government department were to commission a survey of good practice.)

All

29) Review their equal opportunities policies in employment, service delivery and public consultation, and ensure that these refer explicitly to religion as well as to ethnicity, race and culture

The answer is as for recommendation 1.

30) In programmes of grants to voluntary organisations, be sensitive to religious and ethical concerns about the use of National Lottery funds

This does broadly happen.

Education (local education authorities and schools)

31) Use their influence to ensure that local Muslim communities are appropriately represented on schools' governing bodies, particularly schools which have substantial proportions of Muslim pupils

Several local authorities work closely on this subject with forums and liaison committees in their areas. It would be valuable if the DfES were to commission a study of successful practice.

32) Encourage mentoring schemes, particularly in secondary schools, which will provide role models for Muslim pupils

There has been a substantial expansion of mentoring schemes since 1997 and Muslims are involved in many of them. It would be valuable if the DfES were to commission a study of successful practice.

33) Review the definitions of racial harassment used in their policy documentation and programmes of activities, and ensure that explicit reference is made to religion

See the reference to Ealing Education Authority in chapter 8. Several local authorities do refer to religious hostility and Islamophobia in their policy documentation but there is no requirement or even

encouragement to do so from the government or from the CRE.

34) Develop written guidelines on meeting the pastoral, religious and cultural needs of Muslim pupils

Several local authorities have done this. One of the most detailed and helpful was produced in Birmingham in collaboration with Birmingham Central Mosque. In 2002 Education Bradford issued detailed and helpful guidelines for schools on Ramadan and this was nationally available on the website of the Muslim Council of Britain. There is still a great and urgent need for central government to provide guidance.

35) Encourage more Muslims to train as teachers, including for but not only as teachers of religious education

Some local authorities have excellent procedures and systems for encouraging the employment of teachers and classroom assistants from a wide range of communities. One of the most successful is Tower Hamlets. It would be valuable if the DfES were to commission a study of successful practice nationally.

Housing authorities

36) Review the definitions of 'racial harassment' in their policy documentation, and ensure that there is an explicit reference to religion

No information is available nationally. Since harassment aggravated by religious hostility is now recognised formally by the criminal law, most local authorities do now refer to this in their documentation and procedures.

Health care organisations

37) Develop guidelines on good practice in health care relating to religious and cultural needs

No information is available nationally. It would be valuable if a national body were to commission a survey of good practice.

Police forces

38) When recording acts of violence and harassment which appear to be racially motivated, note acts which have a specifically religious dimension, for example desecration of

places of worship, violence accompanied by abuse of religious beliefs and practices, and violence against people wearing distinctively religious dress or symbols

Since the amendment to the Crime and Disorder Act and the statement by the Attorney General in summer 2003 (see chapter 6) this is beginning to happen.

Voluntary and private bodies

Employers, employers' organisations and unions

39) Include references to religion in their equal opportunities statements and policies, and state their opposition to discrimination on religious grounds, both in recruitment and in general personnel management

The EU Employment directive has made these actions mandatory. In addition, the Trades Union Congress issued model rules for its members in 2001 which specifically referred to the need to prevent religious discrimination.

Funding organisations

40) In programmes of grants to voluntary organisations, be sensitive to religious and ethical concerns about the use of National Lottery funds

This is broadly accepted.

National Union of Journalists

41) Complement its statement and guidelines on race reporting with a statement and guidelines about reporting on culture and religion

No specific guidelines have been issued on religion, although the code of conduct in its clause on discriminatory coverage cites creed as one of the areas of concern. See chapter 9 for reference to a code of practice issued in the United States.

Muslim organisations

42) Discuss this report and identify the recommendations on which they themselves can take immediate initiatives

Since 1997 several new Muslim organisations have been created at national and local levels and existing organisations have been strengthened. They have been

active in opposing Islamophobia across a wide range of policy areas.

43) Both locally and nationally, press for the implementation of the recommendations in this report

A range of high-profile and skilfully focused campaigns have been launched relating to health, education, the media and the law.

44) Routinely complain to the Press Complaints Commission (PCC) and to the newspapers concerned when they consider that coverage of Islam or of Muslims has been inaccurate, misleading or distorted

Individuals and groups have made specific complaints on specific articles and there have been meetings with senior PCC officials. Concern remains, however, about the PCC guidelines (see chapter 10) since they protect individuals but not groups or communities.

45) Draw up action plans on media relations, and should provide awareness-raising sessions and seminars for journalists

The Muslim Council of Britain (MCB) and the Forum Against Islamophobia and Racism (FAIR), amongst others, have been active in monitoring media coverage of Islam and in organising forceful complaints. The MCB has held a serious of meetings with national newspaper editors.

46) Make common cause with non-Muslim organisations to secular bodies, at local as well as national levels

Muslim groups and individuals now participate in a number of cross faith and non-faith organisations, including the United Britain Trust. Muslim organisations were heavily involved in mass anti-war demonstrations before and during the conflict with Iraq. The Uniting Britain Trust published a valuable survey of Muslim-Jewish contacts and collaboration (Hurst and Nasir, 2003).

Non-Muslim faith communities

47) Leaders to accept that they have a major responsibility for reducing Islamophobia, and for giving no encouragement to it in any way

The present Archbishop of Canterbury gave a major lecture on inter-faith relations in summer 2003 and the previous Archbishop worked hard to cultivate relations with Muslim and other faiths. The Lambeth group (convened by Archbishop George Carey for the millennium) has continued its work and out of it has come the faiths team in the race equality unit at the Home Office (see above at note 27). The Church of England has a national officer working on Christian-Muslim relations with a working party of Christians and Muslims, exploring appropriate structures for joint faith work.

48) Routinely complain to the Press Complaints Commission and to the newspapers concerned when they consider that coverage of Islam or of Muslims has been inaccurate, misleading or distorted

Church organisations have not taken this up in a systematic way. Complaints were made in 2003 when the Oxford Diocesan newspaper, *The Door*, contained some anti-Muslim sentiments in its letters column but the complaints were not published.

49) Appoint officers, at a range of appropriate levels, to be responsible for inter-faith relations, and give them relevant administrative, financial and institutional support

Most church bodies working at national level and some at regional and local levels have inter-faith officers. The Local Government Association, in collaboration with the Inter-Faith Network, has issued comprehensive guidelines to local authorities on working with faith communities, and reference to the involvement of faith based organisations now appears routinely in government and other policies and funding guidelines. Regional development agencies (for example Yorkshire Forward) are actively developing and funding faith-based work, as are learning and skills councils.

50) Discuss Islamophobia directly and incorporate reference to Islamophobia into their guidelines and policy documents

Nationally there is still little reference to Islamophobia in the antiracist programmes and initiatives of the churches. In autumn 2003, however, the Churches' Commission for Racial Justice published *Redeeming the Time: all God's people must challenge racism* and this did contain an extract from the 1997 report of the Commission on British Muslims and Islamophobia. Further, the model policy statement in this publication

made an explicit commitment to combating Islamophobia.

51) Make common cause with Muslim organisations to secular bodies, at local as well as national levels

One good example of this took place in December 2003 when several senior bishops of the Church of England joined with Jewish and Muslim leaders to denounce government policies on internment without trial. (Letters column, *The Guardian*, 13 December and follow-up letter by Jews and Muslims on 16 December). However, such examples are still rare.

Political parties

52) Take measures to increase the likelihood of Muslim candidates being selected in winnable seats at the next general election

There are now two Muslim MPs (both Labour – Mohammad Sarwar in Glasgow Govan and Khalid Mahmood in Birmingham Perry Barr) but complaints persist that Muslim candidates are rarely selected as candidates for winnable seats by the major parties.

53) Propose the appointment of Muslims to the House of Lords

See note 26 above. As of November 2003 there are four Muslims in the House of Lords.

54) Use their influence to increase the representation of British Muslims on public bodies and commissions

There have been more such appointments, but no precise information is available.

Press Complaints Commission

55) Review the wording of its code of practice, and consider modifying and strengthening the statement about avoiding racial and religious discrimination

The statement has not been modified.

Race equality organisations and monitoring groups

56) Address Islamophobia in their programmes of action, for example by advocating and lobbying for the policy and procedural changes included in this list of recommendations

Race equality councils still do not have religion in their formal remit, but many are working to improve relations between Muslims and non-Muslims. Bath and North East Somerset REC, for example, are part of Islamascope, a multi-agency partnership, and are developing a programme to promote good relations between faith communities and to address issues around Islamophobia. In Central Scotland the REC is involved in a project to resolve conflict, defuse tension and bring about greater understanding between people of diverse cultures, religions and ethnic origin.

57) Review the definitions of 'racial harassment' used in their policy documentation, and ensure that there is an explicit reference to religion

There is no information currently available on whether this has been done. It would be valuable if the CRE were to make a survey of this and similar issues.

58) Routinely complain to the Press Complaints Commission and to the newspapers concerned when they consider that coverage of Islam or of Muslims has been inaccurate, misleading or distorted

See note 57 above.

The Runnymede Trust

59) Ensure that the recommendations in this report are brought to the attention of all relevant bodies

The Trust distributed a summary and in due course substantial extracts from the 1997 report were posted for a time on its website.

60) Ensure that actions over the years to implement the recommendations in this report are closely monitored

Monitoring was undertaken by the Commission when it was reconstituted in 1999. Letters were sent to several hundred public bodies and a progress document entitled *Addressing the Challenge of Islamophobia* was compiled in summer 2001. Subsequent publications provided comment and resources responding to 9/11 (*Addressing Prejudice and Islamophobia*, October 2001) and set out the Commission's views on the Race Relations Amendment Act (*Changing Race Relations*, spring 2002).

Priorities, 2004-2010

The sixty notes above, and more especially the discussions in the main body of this report, indicate that a many-pronged approach to combating Islamophobia and to recognising British Muslim identity is required. Legislation and regulation have important parts to play, but so also do ethical and professional codes of practice, the campaigning and lobbying efforts in the voluntary and community sector, and good will amongst individuals.

There are notes below on the principal priorities in the years ahead. Some could be implemented straightaway. Others will necessarily take time.

Central government: immediate priorities

For central government and its agencies (most obviously, the Commission for Racial Equality), an immediate priority is to encourage all public bodies to incorporate a commitment to avoiding religious discrimination in their race equality schemes and policies. Box 38 summarises the kinds of change that should be made to existing documentation. Textually the changes are small, just a matter of adding a few more words. Conceptually, however, they are significant and would provide a valuable basis of further developments. They would mean that public bodies undertake a positive duty to avoid religious discrimination in all their operations, to promote good relations between members of different religious communities, and to provide equality of opportunity between members of different religious communities. Having accepted the positive duty they would incorporate it into their detailed action plans.

Central government departments should also, as mentioned in some of the notes above (see 31, 35, 36 and 37 for examples), commission surveys of good practice at local levels. The DfES study of educational resources about Islam (see note 9) is a good model.

Further, each department should look again at the recommendations made in the 1997 report and consider sympathetically and positively, as distinct from defensively, their response.

Central government: medium term priorities

In the medium term, central government should:

☐ introduce legislation against discrimination on religious grounds in service delivery

☐ make it mandatory as distinct from voluntary for all public bodies to have a positive duty to prevent discrimination on religious grounds, to promote good relations between members of different faith communities and to provide equal opportunities for all regardless of religious affiliation

☐ set up a commission on religion in public life, as recommended by the Commission on the Future of Multi-Ethnic Britain

All organisations

Regardless of whether or not they receive encouragement from the government, as outlined above, all organisations in the private, public and voluntary sectors should place upon themselves a positive duty to avoid discrimination on religious grounds and to promote equality of opportunity for members of all faith communities.

All should look, or look again, at the recommendations made in the 1997 report and consider sympathetically and positively, not defensively, their response.

Regulation, inspection and advice

It is particularly important that that all bodies concerned with regimes of regulation and inspection, and all bodies tasked with providing support and challenge to public institutions, should consider this report and the implications of it for their work.

The media

All organisations, as appropriate, should consider the recommendations in Box 37 of this report:

Box 38

Changing race relations
– amendments to existing documentation

The phrase 'race equality'

The term 'race equality' should generally be expanded so that there is a reference to cultural diversity as well. For example, 'race equality schemes' should be known as 'schemes for race equality and cultural diversity', or as 'equality and diversity schemes'.

The term 'racial group', in most places where it appears in policy documentation, should be expanded so that it reads 'racial, religious or cultural group'.

The term 'racial group' is defined in the official CRE glossary as 'a group of people defined by their race, colour, nationality (including citizenship), ethnic or national origin'. This is a legal meaning that could not possibly be arrived at by common sense. For this reason if for no other, the term 'racial or cultural group' would be substantially clearer. But in view of the increased salience of religion and belief in race relations, and of the fundamental significance of language in cultural identity, the wording in the glossary should be expanded, so that it reads as follows:

Racial or cultural group
Means a group of persons defined by their race, colour, nationality (including citizenship), religion or belief, language, ethnic or national origins.

Monitoring

Public bodies should be required or encouraged to monitor by religious affiliation as well as by ethnicity. The categories should be those that were used in the 2001 Census.

Source: Changing Race Relations, published by the Commission on British Muslims and Islamophobia, 2002

NOTES AND SOURCES

Chapter 1

1   Speech by Home Office minister Fiona Mactaggart, 18 December 2003. The wider context for her speech included the hijab controversy in France. Well-publicised statements deploring developments in France were also made by Robin Cook, the former Foreign Secretary, and Dr Rowan Williams, the Archbishop of Canterbury. For other quotations from statements by government ministers about Islam and British Muslims see the CD Rom prepared in 2003 by the Foreign and Commonwealth Office, *Think Again: an information resource for the British Muslim communities*.

2   All quotations from individuals in this chapter are from interviews conducted by Hugh Muir and Laura Smith in November 2003, or else from written statements that some of the interviewees subsequently made.

Chapter 2

1   See for example Noorad (2002), Sardar and Davies Chapter 3 (2002), Halliday (2002) and Said (1987).

2   In particular see Allen and Nielsen (2002).

3   There are examples in Allen and Nielsen (2002), and on the websites of the Forum Against Islamophobia and Racism, the Islamic Human Rights Commission and *The Muslim News*.

4   This particular insult was made by Denis MacShane MP, minister of state at the Foreign and Commonwealth Office, in November 2003. It was compounded by the feebleness of his apology a few days later. See, for example, Kamal Ahmed (2003).

5   *Daily Mail*, 5 October 2001, cited in Villate-Compton (2002). See also Yarde (2001), who writes: I groan inwardly every time I read a headline in the popular press about our asylum 'crisis'. I don't need to read the text, I've read the story a hundred times: same words, same message, repackaged according to the demon of the day, then regurgitated as if the use of the same tired old metaphors were something new.' The latest demon of the day, she adds, is Muslims.

6   Norman Tebbit, *The Spectator*, 27 April 2002.

7   *The Muslim Weekly*, 5-11 December 2003, p.11. The text on the poster read 'Ali did not tell us his real name or his true nationality. He was arrested and sent to prison for 12 months.' This statement was translated into five languages, all of them connected with Muslim countries. A detailed legal reference was given in small print but in fact the case that was cited had nothing to do with asylum and nationality claims.

8   One of the five examples was about a legal case that was *sub judice* at the time. A British Muslim had been arrested and charged but not yet tried or convicted.

9   Kilroy-Silk (2004). The author's belief that Iran is an Arab country meant that the article appeared to be an attack on Muslims as well as on Arabs.

10   There is further discussion in chapter 6. See, for example, the quotations in Box 16.

11   Presidential address at General Synod, York, 14 July 2003.

12   The sense of being under siege is global, not confined to Britain: see Akbar Ahmed (2003).

13   Modood (2002).

14   Davies (2002).

15   Most recently, see Lewis (2002) and Lewis (2003).

16   Huntington (1997), pp 217-18.

17   Cox and Marks (2002) provide substantial and sympathetic discussion of American views.

18   See, for example, Alticriti (2003) about statements made by the US under-secretary of defence for intelligence, Lieutenant-General William (Gerry) Boykin. Boykin had said that the US war on terror is a spiritual battle between a Christian nation and Satan, and that God had chosen George Bush to be president. Talking about a Muslim leader whom he had met in Somalia and who had claimed Allah's protection, Boykin said he was confident that such protection would be ineffective since 'I knew my god was bigger than his. I knew that my god was a real god and his was an idol'.

19   In the usual translations from the original, Pope Urban II when launching the Crusades at the Council of Clermont in 1095 declared: 'What a disgrace if a race so despicable, degenerate and enslaved by demons should overcome a people endowed with faith in almighty God and resplendent in the name of Christ!'

20   Said (1987).

21   Runnymede (2000), pp 61-62. Halliday (2002) proposes the term 'anti-Muslimism'.

22   For example, Brendan MacAllister, director of Mediation Northern Ireland. There is further reference to his work in chapter 9.

23   For example, in Commission on the Future of Multi-Ethnic Britain (2000), especially chapter 5.

24   Clegg and Leichty (2001). There is fuller information at www.corrymeela.org.

25   An-Nisa Society is a women's organisation working for the welfare of the Muslim family, with a special focus on the needs of women, children and young people. Established in 1985, it has led the way in promoting a British Muslim identity and the development of Islam-centred services. Publications include An-Nisa Society (1992, 1996, 1999), Basit (1999) and articles and lectures by Khalida Khan (1999, 2002) and Humera Khan (2002). Some of the Society's concerns about the position of Muslim women are reflected in Shah-Kazemi (2001) and about mental health in Skinner (2001).

26   An-Nisa Society (1992), UKACIA (1993).

27   *Q News* developed from the publications *Muslim Voice* and *Muslim Wise*.

28   Khan (1999).

29   Bodi (1999). More recently, the chairman of the CRE has made several high-profile statements opposing Islamophobia. See for example Ahmed (2003), 'Macshane faces anger of racial equality chief', concerning remarks by a minister about British Muslims, referred to above in note 4.

30   Hansard for 28 April 1976 and 4 May 1976 , cited in Hepple and Chaudhury (2001), p.3.

31   See for example Commission on British Muslims and Islamophobia (2002)

32   The idea of adapting the Macpherson definition of institutional racism to Islamophobia was developed by a range of Muslim organisations, including the An-Nisa Society. The first two quotations in Box 9 are from submissions to the Stephen Lawrence Inquiry. The third was formulated by Sir William Macpherson and his advisers. The fourth appears in *Redeeming the Time*, a policy document issued in 2003 by the Churches Commission for Racial Justice.

Chapter 3

1   All major statements by the Archbishop are archived at www.archbishopofcanterbury.org/serpns-speeches.

2   For fuller discussions of Islamophobia and westophobia, and of the international situation since 11 September 2001, see Abukhalil (2002), Ahmed (2003), Tariq Ali (2002), Ameli (2002), Berman (2003), Cox and Marks (2003) Esposito (2002), Halliday (2002), Hoge and Rose (2001), Hussain (new edition 2003), Bernard Lewis (2002, 2003), Malik (2002, 2003), Noor (1997), Noorani (2002), Said (1987 with new introduction 2003 and 1981 with new introduction 1997), Sardar and Wyn Davies (2002) and Scruton (2002).

3   Yasmin Alibhai-Brown, *The Independent*, 5 November 2001

4   Henry Porter, *The Observer*, 14 October 2001

5   For a magisterial review of the new international situation, broadly sympathetic to the current American administration, see *The Sword of Achilles* by Philip Bobbitt.

6   Websites presenting the neo-conservative view of world affairs include Americans for Victory over Terrorism at www.avot.org and Patriots for the Defense of America at http://defenseofamerica.org. There is a list of sites critical of American policy at www.guardian.co.uk/antiwar.

7   This is a recurring theme in Edward Said's writings (for example, 1981 and 1987). See also Sardar and Wyn Davies (2002).

Chapter 4

1   The legislation in question was an amendment to the Crime and Disorder Act made as a consequence of the Anti-Terrorism, Crime and Security Act 2001. It is discussed in chapter 5.

2   Kelly (2004)

3   Ahmed (2003), pp. 18-19.

4   In addition to Ahmed (2003), texts by Muslims which urge interaction and dialogue with the West include works by Arkoun (2002), Ramadan (1999 and 2003), Sachedina (2001), Sajid 2001, 2003a, 2003b) and Seddon *et al* (2003).

5   Ziauddin Sardar (2003b)

6   Sardar (2003b)

7   Parekh (2000), pp.337-38.

Chapter 5

1   *No Place Like Home* by Gary Younge, Picador 2000.

2   See, for example, Modood (2003), Taylor (1993) and Vertovec (2002).

3   For a detailed account of the campaigns see Sherif (2001). A key role was played in the 1990s by UK Action Committee on Islamic Affairs (UKACIA), the forerunner of the Muslim Council of Britain.

4   Further cross-tabulations of religious affiliation and social exclusion are to be published during 2004 and will be reported by, amongst others, the Muslim Council of Britain.

Chapter 6

1   Allen and Nielsen (2002)

2   Interview with Hugh Muir, summer 2003

3   Quoted in Ahmed *et al* (2001) from the BNP website. The leaflets were subsequently removed.

4   Dawkins (2001).

5   Islamophobia, it follows, is similar to antisemitism and sectarianism. There is fuller discussion of this point in chapter 4.

6   Anwar and Baksh (2003), pp. 34-36.

7   Amnesty (2003), reported in Oliver and Travis (2003). Substantial publicity was also given in December 2003 to remarks about the ATCSA by the Archbishop of Canterbury (for example, Bates, 2003). There is extensive information about campaigns and protests at www.ihrc.org.uk.

8   There was a particularly outrageous incident in November 2003, when a British Muslim was detained at Heathrow airport. He was one of the most respected and prominent Muslim scholars and leaders in the UK, Shaykh Suleman Motala, and was on his way to a pilgrimage. For more information see *The Muslim News*, editorial article for November 2003, and comment and coverage at www.mcb.org.uk.

9   See Allen (2003) for full discussion.

10   Cited in Anwar and Bakhsh (2003), p. 38.

11   Two reports about the prison service have been published by the Commission for Racial Equality (2003a, 2003b). The second includes a reprint of the first.

12   David Wilson, professor of criminology at the University of Central England. See Wilson (2003) and Prasad (2003).

13   Quoted in Prasad (2003).

14   The list that follows is derived from documentation provided by the Office of the Muslim Adviser in the Prison Service. The items are all being addressed at the level of policy and have the backing of senior management.

Chapter 7

1   Aziz (2003).

2   Paragraph 229 of the UK 13th periodic report to the UN, summer 1999, cited in Commission on the Future of Multi-Ethnic Britain (2000), paragraph 17.7. Notable proposals to amend UK legislation were made in private bills by John Austin MP (*Hansard* for 3 March 1998) and Lord Ahmed (28 October 1999).

3   There is full information on the website of the Department for Trade and Industry, www.dti.gov.uk/er/equality.

4   The word in the legislation is belief. But the regulations make clear that 'this includes a person's *supposed* religious belief or political opinion [emphasis added] and the absence of any, or any particular, religious belief or political opinion'. The emphasis is on community affiliation, or assumed affiliation, not on the espousal of any religious doctrines.

5   Valuable draft guidance was published by ACAS in autumn 2003. From a Muslim point of view, it contained several weaknesses, as outlined by the British Muslim Research Centre (2003).

Chapter 8

1   For further discussions and notes about British Muslim identity see the special section on the website of *The Muslim News* and the 'Muslim Voices' pages at *The Guardian*. Books on this theme include those by Ameli (2002) and Shain (2003).

2   See the discussion in chapter 6 and a major article on Muslim youth by Yahya Birt, 'Being a Real Man in Islam: drugs, criminality and the problem of masculinity', available on the internet.

3   Bhattacharyya *et al* (2003).

4   This was shown in chapter 5. There is fuller information in Cabinet Office (2003) and White (2002). On all indices of poverty, Bangladeshi and Pakistani people in Britain are severely disadvantaged.

5   Emphasised in, for example, a lecture by the chief inspector for schools in England: see Bell (2003).

6   For fuller critiques of the community cohesion reports see chapter 9.

7   Ealing Education Department (2003).

8   See in particular NASUWT (2003). Guidelines were also published in the journal *Race Equality Teaching*, summer 2003 (referred to in one of the stories in Box 26).

Chapter 9

1   Brown (2001a). The interview itself was reported in Brown (2001b). Three days later the Home Secretary was reported as confirming that 'the interview was an accurate reflection of what I said. It's a reflection of what I have been saying for 20 years' (Waugh, 2001).

2   Cantle (2001), Clark (2001), Home Office (2001) and Ritchie (2001).

3   There are also thirteen 'shadow pathfinders'. Further details are at www.communitycohesion.gov.uk.

4   A leading specialist from Northern Ireland was invited by Oldham Metropolitan Council in 2002 to act as a consultant for its community cohesion policies and programmes. The same person – Brendan McAllister, director of Mediation Northern Ireland – was invited by the Home Office to give the keynote address at a national conference on community cohesion in Leeds in autumn 2003. For his part, McAllister declared a major intellectual debt to Jean Paul Lederach, based in the United States.

5   *News of the World*, 5 March 1989, quoted in Villate-Compton (2002). See also the critique by Ali Rattansi of what he calls 'the new assimilationism' underlying the community cohesion agenda (Rattansi, 2002) and criticisms by Farzana Shain (2003) and Faisal Bodi (2002). Berkeley (2002) criticises the lack of theorising in the Cantle and Denham reports and the absence of serious debate about their concepts and proposals.

6   For example, Bodi (2002).

7   Khan (2002).

8   Ahmed *et al* (2001).

9   Commission on the Future of Multi-Ethnic Britain (2000)

10   There was a similar emphasis on ignorance as a sufficient explanation in the follow-up report of autumn 2003. Debate about the disturbances in northern cities, it was said in the opening paragraph, 'identified the lack of understanding and common ground between communities as a significant cause of the disturbances' (Home Office, 2003). In point of fact, as many observers have complained, there has been very little debate. McAllister's lecture at Leeds was a significant new development.

11   Galtung famously distinguishes between physical violence on the one hand and structural and cultural violence on the other. The latter is close to the concept of institutional Islamophobia. He distinguishes also between physical violence used by the powerful and physical violence by the powerless. The latter is described in Box 30 as 'the violence of the violated'. For fuller explanation of the triangle model see for example Galtung (1998) on the Transcend website at www.transcend.org.

12   The popularity of the contact hypothesis, writes Connolly, can 'be understood in terms of both its simplicity and its underlying political ideology.' He adds that it 'rules out any analysis of the broader social processes, institutions and structures that help to create and sustain racial and ethnic divisions. It is therefore not surprising that the contact hypothesis and its variants should be a particularly popular idea within Government circles' (Connolly, 2000).

13   The point is made by Miles Hewstone (2003).

14   The quotation and following discussion are from Hewstone (2003).

15   On holistic approaches to reducing prejudice and intolerance amongst adolescents and young adults see for example the research sponsored by the Home Office (Sibbitt, 1997), summarised in Richardson and Miles (2003.)

16   Home Office (2003), p.12.

Chapter 10

1   There is detailed information in Bunglawala (2002a and 2002b).

2   Bunglawala (2002a).

3   Bunglawala (2002a).

4   The website of the Muslim Council of Britain (www.mcb.org.uk) has several examples of letters of complaint sent to national newspapers and the Press Complaints Commission, and of dismissive and unhelpful replies.

5   All documented in Muslim Council of Britain (2002).

6   If such a code had been in existence, the article by Robert Kilroy-Silk in the *Express on Sunday*, 4 January 2004, would almost certainly not have been published. All Arabs, he said, are 'suicide bombers, limb-amputators, women-repressors'. Substantial pressure was mobilised by organisations such as the Muslim Council of Britain, the Islamic Society of Britain, the Muslim Association of Britain and the Muslim Public Affairs Committee and this was well supported by the CRE. Mr Kilroy-Silk and the *Sunday Express* issued an apology. Nevertheless the BBC cancelled Mr Kilroy-Silk's contract.

7   Whitaker (2002). The website is at www.al-bab.com.

8   For Muslim views of antisemitism see Ball (2002) and Bhatia (2003), and on Islamophobic media coverage of the Middle East in relation to Israel see articles and press releases at www.mcb.org.uk. On contacts and cooperation between British Muslims and British Jews see Hurst and Nisar (2003).

BIBLIOGRAPHY

(All publishers are in London, except where indicated)

AbuKhalil, As 'ad (2002) *Bin Laden, Islam, and America's New 'War on Terrorism'*, New York: Seven Stories Press

Afshar, Haleh (2003) In Two Minds, in Voluntary Service Overseas, *Cultural Breakthrough: essays*, VSO

Ahmed, Akbar (2003) *Islam under Siege: living dangerously in a post-honor world*, Cambridge: Polity Press

Ahmed, Kamal (2003) Macshane Faces Anger of Racial Equality Chief, *The Observer*, 23 November

Ahmed, Nafeez and Faisal Bodi, Raza Kazim and Massoud Shadjareh (2001) *The Oldham Riots: discrimination, deprivation and communal tension in the United Kingdom*, Islamic Human Rights Commission

Allen, Christopher (2003) *Fair Justice: the Bradford disturbances, the sentencing and the impact*, Forum Against Islamophobia and Racism

Allen, Christopher and Jørgen Nielsen (2002) *Summary Report on Islamophobia in the European Union after 11 September 2001*, Vienna: European Monitoring Centre on Racism and Xenophobia

Ali, Monica (2003) *Brick Lane*, Doubleday

Ali, Tariq (2002) *The Clash of Fundamentalisms: crusades, jihads and modernity*, Verso

Alibhai-Brown, Yasmin (2001) We British Muslims Must Reclaim Our Faith from the Fanatics, *The Independent*, 5 November

Alticriti, Anas (2003) Silence Speaks Volumes, *The Guardian*, 27 October

Ameli, Saied Reza (2002) *Globalisation, Americanisation and British Muslim Identity*, ICAS Press

Amnesty International UK (2003) *Justice Perverted under the Anti-Terrorism, Crime and Security Act 2001*, Amnesty

Annan, Kofi (2004) *State of the World, Brotherhood and Man*, New York: United Nations

An-Nisa Society (1997) *Developing Health Work for the Muslim Community in Stonebridge*, An-Nisa

An-Nisa Society (1996) *Drugs and Muslims: a report conducted in the Harlesden City Challenge Area*, An-Nisa

An-Nisa Society (1992) *A Muslim Response to the Second Review of the Race Relations Act 1976*, An-Nisa and Q News

Anwar, Mohammed and Qadir Bakhsh (2003) *British Muslims and State Policies*, Warwick: Centre for Research in Ethnic Relations

Arkoun, Mohammed (2002) *The Unthought in Contemporary Islamic Thought*, Saqi Books with the Institute of Ismaili Studies

Aziz, Mohammed (2003a) Envisioning Religious Equality in Britain over the Next Ten Years, *Equal Opportunities Review*, January

Aziz, Mohammed (2003b) Equality and Diversity in Modern Britain: the Muslim perspective, *Connections*, Commission for Racial Equality, February

Aziz, Mohammed (2003c) One Dimensional Race Only Report on Labour Market, *The Muslim News*, November

Ball, Lamaan (2002) *Islam, Muslims and Antisemitism*, Muslim Council of Britain (www.mcb.org.uk/anti-semitism.html)

Basit, Meher, ed. (1999) *Islamic Counselling: papers for an information seminar*, An-Nisa Society

Beckford, James and Sophie Gilliat-Ray (1998) *Religion in Prison: equal rites in a multi-faith society*, Cambridge: Cambridge University Press

Bell, David (2003) *Access and Achievement in Urban Education: ten years on*, Fabian Society

Berkeley, Rob (2002) Foreword, in Runnymede Trust, *Cohesion, Community and Citizenship*, The Runnymede Trust

Berman, Paul (2003) *Terror and Liberalism*, W.W.Norton

Bhatia, Amir (2003) *The Fight Against Antisemitism and Islamophobia: bringing communities together*, Brussels: EU Directorate-General for Employment and Social Affairs

Bhattacharyya, Gargi, Lisa Ison and Maud Blair (2003) *Minority Ethnic Achievement and Progress in Education and Training: the evidence*, Department for Education and Skills

Birt, Yahya (2001) Being a Real Man in Islam: drugs, criminality and the problem of masculinity, http://homepage.ntlworld.com/masud/ISLAM/misc/drugs.htm

Bodi, Faisal (2002) Muslims Got Cantle, What They Needed Was Scarman, *The Guardian*, 1 July

Bodi, Faisal (1999) Is There Life After Macpherson? *Q News*, March

British Muslim Research Centre (2003) *Religion or belief in the workplace: comments on draft guidance*, BMRC

Brown, Colin (2001a) Blunkett's 'British Test' for Immigrants, *Independent on Sunday*, 9 December

Brown, Colin (2001b) Interview with David Blunkett, *Independent on Sunday*, 9 December

Bunglawala, Inayat (2003) Don't Let the Evil of Extremism Taint Islam's Good Name, *The Daily Telegraph*, 17 September

Bunglawala, Inayat (2002a) British Muslims and the Media, in Muslim Council of Britain, *The Quest for Sanity*, pp 43-52.

Bunglawala, Inayat (2002b) It's Getting Harder To Be A British Muslim, *The Observer*, 19 May

Bunt, Gary (2004) *Islam in the Digital Age: online fatwas*, Pluto Press

Burnett, Jonathan (2004) Community, Cohesion and the State, *Race and Class*, January

Cabinet Office Strategy Unit (2003) *Ethnic Minorities and the Labour Market*, Cabinet Office

Cantle, Ted chair (2001) *Community Cohesion: a report of the independent review team*, Home Office

Churches' Commission for Racial Justice (2003) *Redeeming the Time: all God's people must challenge racism*, Churches Together in Britain and Ireland

Clark, Tony chair (2001) *Burnley Speaks, Who Listens?* Burnley Metropolitan Council

Clegg, Cecilia and Joe Leichty (2001) *Moving Beyond Sectarianism*, Belfast: The Corrymeela Community

Coles, Maurice Irfan (2004) *Education and Islam: a new strategic approach*, Leicester: School Development Support Agency

Commission for Racial Equality (2003a) *The Murder of Zahid Mubarek*, Commission for Racial Equality

Commission for Racial Equality (2003b) *Racial Equality in Prisons*, Commission for Racial Equality

Commission on British Muslims and Islamophobia (1997) *Islamophobia, a challenge for us all*, Runnymede Trust

Commission on British Muslims and Islamophobia (2001), *Addressing the Challenge of Islamophobia: progress report, 1999-2001*, Uniting Britain Trust

● BIBLIOGRAPHY

Commission on the Future of Multi-Ethnic Britain (2000), *The Future of Multi-Ethnic Britain: the Parekh Report,* Profile Books

Connolly, Paul (2000) What Now for the Contact Hypothesis? – towards a new research agenda, *Race Ethnicity and Education,* vol. 3 no.2, June

Cook, Robin (2003) France need not fear schoolgirls in headscarves, *The Independent,* 19 December

Council of Europe (2000) *Combating Intolerance and Discrimination Against Muslims,* 27 April

Cox, Caroline and John Marks (2003) *The 'West', Islam and Islamism: is ideological Islam compatible with liberal democracy?* Civitas

Cross-Party Working Group on Religious Hatred (2002) *Tackling Religious Hatred,* Edinburgh: Scottish Executive

Crown Prosecution Service (2003a) *Guidance on Prosecuting Cases of Racist and Religious Crimes,* CPS

Crown Prosecution Service (2003b) *Racist And Religious Crime – CPS Prosecution Policy,* CPS

Davies, Merryl Wyn (2002) Wilful Imaginings, *New Internationalist,* no. 345, May

Dawkins, Richard (2001) Children Must Choose Their Beliefs, *The Observer,* 30 December

Department of Health (2003) *NHS Chaplaincy: meeting the religious and spiritual needs of patients and staff,* Department of Health

Ealing Education Authority (2003) *Preventing and Addressing Racism in Schools,* London Borough of Ealing

Esposito, John (2002) *Unholy War: terror in the name of Islam,* Oxford University Press

European Centre for Work and Society (2001) *Situation of Islamic Communities in Five European Cities,* Vienna: European Monitoring Centre on Racism and Xenophobia

European Monitoring Centre (2002) *The Fight Against Antisemitism and Islamophobia: bringing communities together,* Vienna: European Monitoring Centre on Racism and Xenophobia

European Monitoring Centre (2002) *Racism and Cultural Diversity in the Mass Media,* Vienna: European Monitoring Centre on Racism and Xenophobia

Fukuyama, Francis (2001) The Real Enemy, New York: *Newsweek,* special issue, December

Galtung, Johan (1998) *Reconstruction, Reconciliation, Resolution: coping with visible and invisible effects of war and violence,* Transcend (www.transcend.org)

Gopin, Marc (2002) *Holy War, Holy Peace: how religion can bring peace to the Middle East,* Oxford University Press

Gopin, Marc (2000) *Between Eden and Armageddon: the future of world religions, violence and peacemaking,* Oxford University Press

Haddock, Maureen (2003) *Community Cohesion Initiatives in Oldham Primary Schools,* Oldham Metropolitan Borough Council

Halliday, Fred (2002) *Two Hours that Shook the World,* IB Tauris

Hansen, Randall (2003) Measures of Integration, *Connections,* Commission for Racial Equality, summer

Haque, Zubaida (2000) The Ethnic Minority 'Underachieving' Group? – investigating the claims of 'underachievement' amongst Bangladeshi pupils in British secondary schools, *Race Ethnicity and Education,* vol. 3 no.2, June

Henzell-Yhomas, Jeremy (2002) *The Challenge of Pluralism and the Middle Way of Islam,* Association of Muslim Social Scientists

Hepple, Bob and Tufyal Choudhury (2001) Tackling Religious Discrimination: practical implications for policy-makers and legislators, Home Office Research Study 221

Hershberg, Eric and Kevin Moore (2002) *Critical Views of September 11: analyses from around the world,* New York: The New Press

Hertsgaard, Mark (2002) *The Eagle's Shadow: why America fascinates and infuriates the world,* Bloomsbury Publishing

Hewstone, Miles (2003) Intergroup Contact: panacea for prejudice? *The Psychologist,* vol.16 no.7, July

Hitchens, Peter (2002) Can We No Longer Even Argue with a Muslim? *Mail on Sunday,* 27 October

Hoge, James and Gideon Rose (2001) *How Did This Happen?* Oxford: Public Affairs Ltd

Home Office (2003a) *Community Cohesion Pathfinder programme: the first six months,* Home Office

Home Office (2003b) *Building a Picture of Community Cohesion: a guide for local authorities and their partners,* Home Office

Home Office (2001) *Building Cohesive Communities: a report of the ministerial group on public order and community cohesion,* Home Office

Hurst, Fiona and Mohammed Nisar (2003) *Positive Contacts between British Muslims and Jews: a model of good practice for all British communities,* Aliph-Aleph UK and Uniting Britain Trust

Hussain, Asad (2003 new edition) *Western Conflict with Islam,* Leicester: Volcano

Imran, Muhammad and Elaine Miskell (2003) *Citizenship and Muslim Perspectives: teachers sharing ideas,* Birmingham: Development Education Centre

Inter-Faith Network (2003a) *Local Inter faith Activity in the UK: a survey,* Inter-Faith Network

Inter-Faith Network (2003b) *Partnerships for the Common Good: interfaith structures and local government,* Inter Faith Network

Inter-religious and International Federation of World Peace (2002) *Islam and the Future of World Peace: proceedings of the World Summit of Muslim leaders,* Tarrytown, New York: IIFWP

Inter-religious and International Federation of World Peace (2003) *State of the Muslim World Today : proceeding of the world summit of Muslim leaders,* Tarrytown, New York: IIFWP

Johnston, Douglas ed. (2003) *Faith-based Diplomacy: trumping realpolitik,* Oxford University Press

Karam, Azza, ed. (2004) *Transitional Political Islam: globalisation, ideology and power,* Pluto Press

Kelly, Elinor (2004) Integration, Assimilation and Social Inclusion: questions of faith, *Policy Futures in Education,* vol.2 no. 1, March

Khan, Humera (2002) The Next Intifada, *Q News,* July/August

Khan, Khalida (2002) Healing the Self: towards a faith-centred pproach to mental health for the Muslim community, conference presentation, 1 October, An-Nisa Society

Khan, Khalida (1999) Where's the Muslim in Macpherson's Black and White Britain?, *Q News,* February

Kundnani, Arun (2001) *From Oldham to Bradford: the violence of the violated,* Institute of Race Relations

Kundnani, Arun (2002) *An Unholy Alliance? – racism, reigion and communalism, Institute of Race Relations*, 30 July

Lederach, John Paul (1998) Bcyond Violcncc: building sustainable peace, in Eugene Weiner, ed, *The Handbook of Interethnic Coexistence*, New York: Continuum Publishing, pp. 236-245

Lewis, Bernard (2003) *The Crisis of Islam: holy war and unholy terror*, Weidenfeld and Nicolson

Lewis, Bernard (2002) *What went wrong?-western impact and middle eastern response*, Phoenix

Lewis, Philip (2002) Between Lord Ahmed and Ali G: which future for British Muslims?, in Shahid, W.A.R. and P.S. van Koningsfeld, eds, *Religious Freedom and the Neutrality of the State: the position of Islam in the European Union*, Leuven: Peeters

Local Government Association (2002) Guidance on Community Cohesion, LGA

Luton Borough Council (2003) *Sticking Together, Embracing Diversity: report of the community cohesion scrutiny panel*, Luton

Malik, Aftab Ahmad, ed. (2003) *The Empire and the Crescent: global implications for a new American century*, Bristol: Amal Press

Malik, Aftab Ahmad, ed. (2002) *Shattered Illusions: analysing the war on terror*, Bristol: Amal Press

Malik, Iftikhar (2004) *Islam and Modernity: Muslims in Europe and the United States*, Pluto Press

McAllister, Brendan (2003) Mediation and Community Cohesion, address to Home Office Pathfinder Conference, Leeds, 27 November

McLaughlin, Sean (2004) *Representing Muslims*, Pluto Press

McManus, Jim (2001) *Friends or Strangers? – faith communities and community safety*, National Association for the Care and Rehabilitation for Offenders

McTernan, Oliver (2003) *Violence in God's Name: religion in an age of conflict*, Darton, Longman and Todd

Modood, M.S. (2003) *My Faith and I Rest Here*, privately published

Modood, Tariq (2003) Muslims and the Politics of Difference, in Sarah Spencer, ed *The Politics of Migration*, Oxford: Blackwell and *Political Quarterly* 74 (1), pp.100-115

Modood, Tariq (2002a) The Power of Dialogue, in Muslim Council of Britain, *The Quest for Sanity*, pp 112-116.

Modood, Tariq (2002b) Muslims and the Politics of Multiculturalism in Britain, in Hershberg, Eric and Kevin Moore (2002) *Critical Views of September 11: analyses from around the world*, New York: The New Press, pp 193-208.

Muir, Hugh (2003) Mosques Launch Protests over 'Terror' Arrests, *The Guardian*, 13 December

Mukherjee, Bharati (2003) Alien Nation, *Financial Times Magazine*, 13 September

Muslim Council of Britain (2002) *The Quest for Sanity: reflections on September 11 and the aftermath*, Muslim Council of Britain

Muslim Liaison Committee (2001) *Revised Guidelines on Meeting the Religious and Cultural Needs of Muslim Pupils*, Birmingham Central Mosque

National Association of Schoolmasters and Union of Women Teachers (2003) *Islamophobia: advice for schools and colleges*, NASUWT

National Union of Teachers (2003) *The War in Iraq: the impact on schools*, NUT

Noor, Farish ed. (1997) *Terrorising the Truth, Penang*: Just World Trust

Noorani, A G (2002) *Islam and Jihad – prejudice versus reality*, Zed Books

Open Society Institute (2002) *Monitoring Minority Protection in the EU: the situation of Muslims in the UK*, Budapest and New York: Open Society Institute

O'Mohony, Anthoy and Ataullah Siddiqui (2001) eds, *Christians and Muslims in the Commonwealth: a dynamic role in the future*, Altajir World of Islam Trust

O'Sullivan, Jack (2001) Voices behind the Veil, *The Guardian*, 24 September

Ouseley, Herman (2001) *Community Pride Not Prejudice: making diversity work in Bradford*, Bradford: Bradford Vision

Parekh, Bhikhu (2002) Common Belonging, in Runnymede Trust, *Cohesion, Community and Citizenship*, The Runnymede Trust, pp 1-8

Parekh, Bhikhu (2000) *Rethinking Multiculturalism: cultural diversity and political theory*, Basingstoke: Macmillan Press

Poole, Elizabeth (2002) *Reporting Islam: media presentations of British Muslims*, I B Tauris.

Porter, Henry (2001) We Are Right to Fight, *The Observer*, 14 October

Poulter, Sebastian (1990) Towards Legislative Reform of the Blasphemy and Racial Hatred Laws, Public Law, autumn

Prasad, Raekha (2003) No Holds Barred, *The Guardian*, 10 December

Ramadan, Tariq (2003) *Western Muslims and the Future of Islam*, Oxford University Press

Ramadan, Tariq (1999) *To be a European Muslim: a study of Islamic sources in the European context*, Leicester: The Islamic Foundation

Race, Alan (2002) *Religions in Dialogue: from theocracy to democracy*, Aldershot: Ashgate Publishing

Race, Alan (2001) *Interfaith Encounter: the twin tracks of theology and dialogue*, SCM Press

Rattansi, Ali (2002) Who's British? – Prospect and the new assimilationism, in Runnymede Trust, *Cohesion, Community and Citizenship*, The Runnymede Trust, pp 96-105

Richardson, Robin and Berenice Miles (2003) *Equality Stories: recognition, respect and raising achievement*, Stoke on Trent: Trentham

Rifkind, Jeremy (2001) Dialogue is a Necessity, *The Guardian*, 13 November

Ritchie, David chair (2001) *Oldham Independent Review*, Oldham Metropolitan Council

Runnymede (2003) *Developing Community Cohesion: understanding the issues, delivering solutions*, Runnymede Trust

Runnymede (2002) *Cohesion, Community and Citizenship: proceedings of a Runnymede conference*, Runnymede Trust

Sachedina, Abdulaziz (2001) *The Islamic Roots of Democratic Pluralism*, Oxford University Press

● BIBLIOGRAPHY

Sacks, Jonathan (2002) *The Dignity of Difference: how to avoid the clash of civilisations*, Continuum

Said, Edward (1987, reprinted with new introduction 2003) *Orientalism*, Penguin

Said, Edward (1981, reprinted with new introduction 1997) *Covering Islam: how the media and the experts determine how we see the rest of the world*, Vintage

Sajid, Abduljalil (2003a) Islam and Muslims in Europe, lecture in Amaliastraat, Netherlands, 5 March

Sajid, Abduljalil (2003b) The Role and Importance of Interfaith Work, London Borough of Barnet, 16 September

Samad, Yunas (1998) Media and Muslim Identity: intersections of generation and gender, *Innovation*, vol 11 (4), pp 425-438

Sardar, Ziauddin (2003a) Hope and Resistance, *Emel*, November/December

Sardar, Ziauddin (2003b) Cultivating the Soil, *Emel*, September/October

Sardar, Ziauddin and Merryl Wyn Davies (2002) *Why Do People Hate America?* Cambridge: Icon Books

Sardar, Ziauddin, Ashis Nandy and Merryl Wyn Davies (1993) *Barbaric Others: a manifesto on western racism*, Pluto Press

Scruton, Roger (2002) *The West and the Rest: globalisation and the terrorist threat*, Continuum

Seddon, Mohammad Siddique, Dilwar Hussain and Nadeem Malik (2003) *British Muslims: loyalty and belonging*, Leicester: Islamic Foundation

Shah-Kazemi, Sonia (2001) *Untying the Knot: Muslim women, divorce and the Shariah*, Nuffield Foundation and University of Westminster

Shain, Farzana (2003) *The Schooling and Identity of Asian Girls*, Stoke on Trent: Trentham Books

Sherif, Jamal (2001) Campaigning for a Religion Question in the 2001 Census, Muslim Council of Britain (www.mcb.org.uk/census 2001.pdf

Sibbitt, Rae (1997) *The Perpetrators of Racial Harassment and Racial Violence*, Home Office

South Yorkshire Workforce Development Confederation (2003) *Caring for the Spirit: a strategy for the chaplaincy and spiritual healthcare workforce*, Yorkshire: SYWDC

Skinner, Rasjid(2001) Multicultural Issues in Mental Health, conference presentation at Mental Health Collaborative meeting, Harrogate

Stothard, Peter (2003) *30 Days: a month at the heart of Blair's war*, HarperCollins

Taylor, Charles (1993) The Politics of Recognition, in Amy Gutmann, ed., *Multiculturalism and the Politics of Recognition*, Harvard University Press

Thatcher, Margaret (2002) Islamism is the New Bolshevism, *New York Times*, reprinted in *The Guardian*, 12 February

Toynbe, Polly (2001) Last Chance to Speak Out, *The Guardian*, 5 October

UK Action Committee on Islamic Affairs (1993) *Need for Reform: Muslims and the law in multi-faith Britain*, UKACIA

US Department of State (2003) *Fifth Annual Report on Religious Freedom*, Washington, DC

Vertovec, Steven (2002) Islamophobia and Muslim Recognition in Britain, in Yvonne Yazbeck Haddad, ed. *Muslims in the West*, Oxford University Press

Villate-Compton, Pascale (2002) La Menace Sans Visage: images de l'ennemi dans la presse britannique à la suite des attentats du 11 septembre 2001, France: Université de Tours

Waugh, Paul (2001) Blunkett Calls for National Debate on Race and Religion, *The Independent*, 12 December

Weller, Paul and Alice Feldman and Kingsley Purdam (2001) *Religious Discrimination in England and Wales*, Home Office Research Study 220

Wheatcroft, Andrew (2003) *Infidels: the conflict between Christendom and Islam 638-2002*, Viking

Whitaker, Brian (2002) Islam and the British Press, in Muslim Council of Britain, *The Quest for Sanity*, pp 53-57.

White, Amanda (2002) *Social Focus in Brief: ethnicity*, Office of National Statistics

Williams, Rowan (2002) *Writing in the Dust*, Hodder & Stoughton

Wilson, David (2003) *Playing the Game: the experiences of young black men in custody*, Children's Society

Yahmed, Hadi (2003) Islamophobia Escalates in France, *Islam Online*, 17 November

Yarde, Rosalind (2001) Demons of the Day, *The Guardian*, 12 November

Young, Hugo (2001) A Corrosive National Danger in our Multicultural Model, *The Guardian*, 6 November 2001

Younge, Gary (2003) The Wrong Way Round, *The Guardian*, 8 September

ADDRESSES AND WEBSITES

Addresses

Al-Khoei Foundation, Stone Hall, Chevening Road, London NW6 6TN

An-Nisa Society, 85 Wembley Hill Road, Wembley, Middlesex HA9 8BU

Association of Muslim Schools, 512-514 Berridge Road West, Bobbers Mill, Nottingham NG7 5JU

Birmingham Central Mosque, 180 Belgrave Road, Highgate, Birmingham B12 0XS

Bolton Mosques Council fo Community Care, 2-14 Randal Street, Bolton BL3 4AQ

Bradford Council of Mosques, 6 Clarement, Bradford BD7 1BG

British Muslim Research Centre, Office Suite 2, Boardman House, The Broadway, Stratford, London E15 1NG

Centre for the Study of Islam and Christian-Relations, Elmfield House, Selly Oak, Birmingham B29 6LQ

Churches' Commission on Racial Justice, Bastille Court, 2 Paris Garden, London SE1 8ND

Commission for Racial Equality, 201 Borough High Street, London SE1 1GZ

Confederation of Sunni Mosques Midlands, 11 Serpentine Road, Witton, Birmingham B6 6SB

Emel Magazine, 126 The Broadway, London W13 0SY

European Monitoring Centre on Racism and Xenophobia, Rahlgasse 3, A-1060, Vienna

Federation of Students Islamic Societies, 38 Mapesbury Road, London NW12 4JD

Forum Against Islamophobia and Racism, Suite 11, Grove House, 320 Kensal Road, London W10 5BZ

Home Office Faith Communities Unit, 19 Allington Street, London SW1E 5EB

Imams and Mosques Council, 20-22 Creffield Road, London W5 3RP

Impact International, Suite B, 233 Seven Sisters Road, London N4 2BL

Inner Cities Religious Council, 4/110 Eland House, Bressenden Place, London SW1E 5DU

Institute of Muslim Minority Affairs, 46 Goodge Street, London W1P 1EE

Inter-Faith Network for the UK, 8A Grosvenor Place, London SW1W 0EN

Islamic Cultural Centre and London Central Mosque, 146 Park Road, London, NW8 7RG

Islamic Foundation, Ratby Lane, Markfield, Leicestershire LE67 9SY

Islamic Human Rights Commission, PO Box 598, Wembley, Middlesex HA0 4XX

Islamic Society of Britain, 71 Hob Moor Road, Birmingham B10 9AZ

IQRA Trust, 3rd Floor, 16 Grosvenor Crescent, London SW1X 7EP

Jamiat-e-Ulema Britain, 12 Leeds Old Road, Bradford BD3 8HT

Joint Council for the Welfare of Immigrants, 115 Old Street, London EC1V 9RT

Local Government Association, Local Government House, Smith Square, London SW1P 3HZ

London Muslim Coalition, Romney House, Marsham Street, London SW1P 3PY

Lancashire Council of Mosques, Bangor Street Community Centre, Norwich Street, Blackburn BB1 6NZ

Muslim Association of Britain, 233 Seven Sisters Road, London N4 2DA

Muslim Council for Religious and Racial Harmony, 8 Caburn Road, Hove BN3 6EF

Muslim Council of Britain, Suite 5, Boardman House, 64 Broadway, Stratford, London E15 1NT

Muslim Eductional Trust, 130 Stroud Green Road, London N4 3RZ

Muslim News, PO Box 380, Harrow, Middlesex HA2 6LL

Muslim Parliament, 109 Fulham Palace Road, London W6 8JA

Muslim Women Society, 272 Dickenson Road, Longsight, Manchester M13 0YL

Q News, PO Box 4245, London W1A 7YH

Refugee Council, 240-250 Ferndale Road, London SW9 8BB

Runnymede Trust, Suite 106, London Fruit and Wool Exchange, Brushfield Street, London E1 6EP

The Muslim Weekly, 117 Whitechapel Road, London E1 1DT

Uniting Britain Trust, Barakat House, 116-118 Finchely Road, London NW3 5HT

Young Muslim Sisters UK, POBox 7539, Birmingham B10 9AU

Young Muslims UK, 14 Mile Cross Place, Halifax HX1 4HW

Websites

British Muslims

For current issues affecting British Muslims, it is particularly worth visiting::

Forum Against Islamophobia (www.fairuk.org.uk) – valuable news service whereby subscribers receive free of charge, several times a week, a selection of news items

Honest News (www.honestnews.com) – substantial discussions of Islamophobia in the media

Islamic Human Rights Commission (www.ihrc.org) – strong international focus as well as British

Islamic Society of Britain (www.isb.org.uk) – conferences, news and events

Muslim Association of Britain (www.mabonline.net) – comment, news, discussions and articles

Muslim Council of Britain (www.mcb.org.uk) -wide range of comment and useful statistics, frequently and with a weekly newsletter

Muslim Directory (www.muslimdirectory.co.uk) – substantial lists of contacts and links

Muslim News (www.muslimnews.co.uk) – substantial archive of news items, articles and comment

Muslim Public Affairs Committee (www.mpacuk.org) – includes advice on complaints to the media

Muslim Voices pages at the *Guardian* (www.guardian.co.uk/ muslimvoices) – views of international affairs

Q News (www.q-news.com) – brief summaries of key articles over the years

Salaam (www.salaam.co.uk) – wide-ranging data on Islam in Britain

Islamic culture and faith

The sites mentioned above have many links to sites specialising in issues of Islamic faith, culture and spirituality. So do the following:

Council on American-Islamic Relations www.cair-net.org

Islamic Information and Support Centre of Australia www.iisca.org

Islamic Cultural Centre www.islamicculturalcentre.co.uk

Islamic Relief (www.islamic-relief.com)

Islamicity (www.islamicity.com)

Islam Online (www.islamonline.net)

Islamic Awareness Week (www.iaw.org.uk)

Islam for Today (www.islamfortoday.com)

Islam in the United States (www.islam-usa.com)

Islamic Foundation (www.islamic-foundation.org.uk)

Islamic Solutions (www.islamicsolutions.com)

IQRA Trust (www.iqratrust.org.uk)

Masud (www.masud.co.uk)

Mosaic International (www.mosaicinformation.org.uk)

Muslim Educational Trust (www.muslim-ed-trust.org.uk)

Muslim Heritage (www.muslimheritage.com)

Muslim Family Network (www.al-usrah.net)

Ummah (www.ummah.org.uk/what-is-islam)

Ummah News (www.ummahnews.com)

Virtual Classroom ((www.thevirtualclassroom.net)

Young Muslims UK (www.ymuk.net)

Interfaith dialogue and activities

BBC (www.bbc.co.uk/religion)

Centre for the Study of Islam and Christian-Muslim Relations (www.bham.ac.uk/theology/csic)

Interfaith Network for the UK (www.interfaith.org.uk)

Multi-Faith Group for Healthcare Chaplaincy (www.mfghc.com)

Government

Advisory, Conciliation and Arbitration Service (www.acas.org.uk)

Crown Prosecution Service (www.cps.gov.uk)

Faith Communities Unit (www.homeoffice.gsi.gov.uk)

Foreign Office (www.fco.gov.uk)

Inner Cities Religious Council (www.odpm.gov.uk)

Local Government Association (www.lga.gov.uk)

Europe

Collectif Contre l'Islamophobie en France http://islamophobie.net – (in French) useful discussions of current issues and news of campaigns and events

European Monitoring Centre on Racism and Xenophobia (http://eumc.eu.int) – includes links to organisations throughout Europe concerned with combating racism and Islamophobia

Forum of European Muslim Youth and Student Organisations (www.femyso.com) – news of conferences and events

Institute for the Study of Islam in the Modern World (www.isim.ac.ne) – academic articles with a global perspective

Various

Council for the Advancement of Arab-British Relations (www.caabu.org)

Community Cohesion (www.communitycohesion.gov.uk) – national policy and local case studies

Equalities Coalition (www.equalities.org) – news and views on the Single Equality Commission

Just World (www.just-international.org) – based in Malaysia, articles on roots and challenges of Islamophobia

HSBC (www.amanahfinance.hsbc.com) – home finance and banking in accordance with Shariah

National Union of Schoolmasters and Union of Women Teachers (www.nasuwt.org.uk) – guidelines on combating Islamophobia in education

Social Science Research Council (www.ssrc.org/sept11/essays/) – range of academic articles written shortly after 11 September

South Yorkshire Workforce Development Confederation (www.sywdc.nhs.uk) – includes the text of *Caring for the Spirit* on hospital chaplaincy